TEFF LOVE

ADVENTURES IN VEGAN ETHIOPIAN COOKING

Kittee Berns

BOOK PUBLISHING COMPANY

Summertown, Tennessee

Library of Congress Cataloging-in-Publication Data

Berns, Kittee, author.
  Teff love : adventures in vegan Ethiopian cooking / Kittee Berns.
     pages   cm
  Includes index.
  ISBN 978-1-57067-311-5 (pbk.) — ISBN 978-1-57067-887-5 (e-book)
  1. Cooking, Ethiopian.   2. Vegetarian cooking.   I. Title.
  TX725.E84B47 2014
  641.5963—dc23

                                                    2014040191

Color photos: Alan Roettinger, Kittee Berns, Amy Gedgaudas
Food styling: Alan Roettinger, Kittee Berns
Cover and interior design: John Wincek

Printed on recycled paper

Book Publishing Co. is a member of Green Press Initiative. We chose to print this title on paper with post-consumer recycled content, processed without chlorine, which saved the following natural resources:

53 trees
1,662 pounds of solid waste
24,832 gallons of wastewater
4,578 pounds of greenhouse gases
24 million BTUs of total energy

For more information, visit greenpressinitiative.org.

Paper calculations from Environmental Defense Paper Calculator, edf.org/papercalculator.

Printed in Canada

Book Publishing Company
PO Box 99
Summertown, TN 38483
888-260-8458
bookpubco.com

ISBN 13: 978-1-57067-311-5

20   6 7 8 9

Calculations for the nutritional analyses in this book are based on the average number of servings listed with the recipes and the average amount of an ingredient if a range is called for. Calculations are rounded up to the nearest gram. If two options for an ingredient are listed, the first one is used. The analyses include oil used for frying. Not included are optional ingredients and serving suggestions.

CONTENTS

For my double bubs,
Dazee and Vee.

FOREWORD

This book couldn't have come at a better time. As global concerns about diet and its effects on human health and the environment are rapidly spreading worldwide, people everywhere are clamoring for change. Ethiopians, who only a few years ago associated veganism with religious fasting, have also been affected and influenced by this growing awareness. At the same time, the perceptions of Ethiopia are shifting from its legacy of famine and extreme poverty to its rich and exotic culinary heritage. Our tradition of healthful, wholesome, simple yet flavorful and hearty food has encouraged the proliferation of Ethiopian restaurants throughout North America and inspired countless people to try our traditional vegan dishes.

Ethiopians themselves are also gaining a greater awareness about vegan ethics and values. A dramatic development has been the opening of exclusively vegan restaurants in Ethiopia, which is an incredibly positive sign.

In 2008, when there were only a handful of vegans in Ethiopia, I helped establish Vegan Association Ethiopia. It was the first group in the country to champion veganism. Today we are joined by Vegan Ethiopia and International Fund for Africa (IFA). These fledgling organizations have worked tirelessly to spread the word about veganism despite being on a shoestring budget. We host conferences, provide video presentations, and leaflet on behalf of veganism. We educate restaurants and hotels about vegan food. And by partnering with Animals and Us, an Australia-based organization, we are able to provide textbooks, advocate humane education, and teach positive values to children through our Animals' Friends school clubs.

I believe that every vegan has a responsibility to help educate others about veganism, and with this book, Kittee Berns has done more than her part. *Teff Love* is the delicious result of Kittee's love and appreciation of Ethiopian food combined with her creativity, compassion, and commitment to vegan values. It's a vital, priceless gift to vegans and nonvegans alike.

I invite you to let Kittee take you on exciting culinary adventures and travel to Ethiopia by way of her spectacular recipes. Enjoy!

With love,
Mesfin Hailemariam (one of the first and few vegans of Ethiopia)
Founder and Director, Vegan Ethiopia
meshagem@gmail.com

PREFACE

As a fledging vegan in the early nineties, I lived in the DC 'burbs, where restaurants specializing in all sorts of amazing cuisines abounded. I lived with friends who, like me, were interested in exploring delicious vegetarian food, cooking, and related adventures. We ate out as often as we could afford to, and we cooked at home a lot too. However, Ethiopian food was something we always enjoyed at restaurants instead of preparing it ourselves, even though it was everyone's favorite.

It wasn't until I had my own apartment that I first tried my hand at Ethiopian cooking. I threw a small birthday party for a good friend, and made a few pots of veganized Ethiopian fare using recipes cobbled together from the nascent Internet and *Sundays at Moosewood* cookbook. The food turned out really good, but the best part was the fun we had eating it together from large platters with our hands.

When my partner, Dazee, and I moved to New Orleans in 2001, I started cooking Ethiopian dishes regularly. Dining out for vegan food in the Big Easy was a bit more difficult than the name implies, and finding Ethiopian food was even harder, so preparing it at home became a way to celebrate special occasions with lots of friends.

While my experience with and knowledge of Ethiopian food and cooking comes solely from a North American perspective, I'm passionate about and excited by the cuisine and have thrown my heart and belly into learning as much about it as possible. Everything I know has been culled and pieced together from eating Ethiopian food from countless restaurants and food trucks in cities across North America, reading books about Ethiopia, spending hours scouring restaurant menus, going on grocery store treasure hunts, watching Amharic cooking videos, scrutinizing Ethiopian food photographs, and talking to anyone familiar with the cuisine.

If you've never had the opportunity to try Ethiopian food, or if you love it but don't know how to cook it, my hope is that these recipes will demystify it and help transform you into an Ethiopian cooking maven. And if you already have mad Ethiopian kitchen skills and know-how, I'm pretty confident you'll discover new and exciting recipes in this book that you've never seen or tasted before. I also hope this book will help promote and support the vegan community, wherever it may be, here and abroad.

introduction

Ethiopian food may seem exotic, mysterious, and maybe even a bit intimidating if you've never tried your hand at cooking it before. One of the reasons I wrote this book is to show how converting your kitchen into a virtual wot factory is surprisingly simple and grocery-store friendly to boot. You'll discover that most of these recipes are made from easy-to-find unprocessed ingredients, such as whole grains, legumes, vegetables, and spices. They're great for folks with food allergies or intolerances, since most of the recipes are also free of gluten, corn, and soy (or can be made so with easy adaptations).

My priority in creating this book was to fill it with as many practical, delicious recipes as possible. I aimed to include all the familiar dishes you've come to enjoy at your favorite Ethiopian restaurants, but I also wanted to include exciting new recipes that most North Americans probably haven't seen or tasted before. As you read through and prepare these recipes, please bear in mind that this book is not an exhaustive source of vegetarian Ethiopian cooking. Like any country, Ethiopia has a complex culture of regional foods, and the recipes here are those I'm familiar with and that were accessible through my research. In addition, I've avoided recipes that require extensive, unfamiliar processes or that call for ingredients that are costly or extremely difficult to find in North America.

BE A FRIEND AND WASH YOUR HANDS

If you're unfamiliar with Ethiopian food, you should know that meals are often social events and are composed of a variety of dishes with contrasting flavors, colors, and textures, all served together on a large platter perched upon a traditional woven stand or basket called a *mesob*. Underneath the various dishes sits *injera*, a spongy, tangy, fermented, crepe-like bread, that soaks up the yummy sauces from the food that rests upon it.

Instead of using utensils, diners tear off pieces of *injera* and use their right hand to scoop and deliver the various morsels directly into their mouths. If there's any tummy room remaining after all the dishes have been devoured, the succulent *injera* left on the bottom of the platter is also scooped up and eaten. It's one of my favorite parts. Of course, eating by hand isn't required, but I think it's a large part of what makes

Ethiopian food enjoyable and special, so my advice is to wash your hands, give it a try, and see what you think; you can always use a fork if that's more your style.

THE HEART OF THE BOOK

No doubt you'll want to get to the heart of this book—the recipes—right away. In general, the recipes in this book can be grouped into four broad categories:

1. Popular vegetarian "fasting" dishes served on veggie combo platters (*bey-aynetu*) in restaurants all over North America. (So you can easily find these recipes in the book, they're marked with this "Veggie Combo Classic" logo.)

2. Lesser known but still traditional vegetarian fasting dishes uncommon in North American restaurants.

3. Dishes my friend Hirut has dubbed "new Ethiopian recipes," which are those I've veganized or put a creative spin on to round out this collection to its fullest level of awesome.

4. "Fusion" recipes, which contain traditional Ethiopian flavors that are added to nontraditional foods.

HOW TO SERVE ETHIOPIAN FOOD

Serving Ethiopian food at home can be as simple or creative as you want to make it. The standard approach is to line a large, flat platter or baking sheet with a single layer of *injera* (cranny-side up to catch the sauce) and spoon the dishes artfully on top. Be sure to serve extra *injera* on the side for each person, and dig in with clean hands. Here are some ideas to add a bit of flair to your presentation:

- Put the *injera* on a large, flat plate and fold the edges over to form a square. Then ladle the dishes on top.

- Cut the *injera* into large shapes, such as rectangles or triangles. Arrange them on a platter and spoon the dishes on top.

- In restaurants, a main dish or leafy salad is usually positioned in the center of the platter, with each other dish spooned symmetrically around it in two different places. Feel free to get as creative with this as you want. Consider the *injera* your edible canvas.

- The easiest way to serve extra *injera* is to fold it in quarters and stack it on an extra plate that's passed around the table as everyone eats. You can also roll the *injera* into tight coils and then cut it into manageable sections. Stack the sections on an extra plate or arrange them around the perimeter of the platter, within easy reach of everyone at the table. Alternatively, arrange the sliced coils so they're sticking out from the platter, similar to the petals of a flower.

A VERY BRIEF HISTORY OF ETHIOPIA

Ethiopia is a northeast African country, and along with Eritrea, Somalia, and the Republic of Djibouti, it makes up the largest portion of the Horn of Africa. Composed of many different religious groups, including Muslims, Jews, and Christians, Ethiopia has a strong culture surrounding vegetarian food (one of religious abstinence rather than ethical vegetarianism).

The country's religious majority follows the Ethiopian Orthodox Church (related to the Coptic Church), which observes fasts for more than two hundred days out of the year. During these periods (Wednesdays, Fridays, and longer durations surrounding specific holidays), the religious abstain from food until late afternoon. Fasts are broken with *ye'tshom megib*, or fasting food, which is required to be free from animal ingredients, although honey and occasionally fish are allowed. Outside of these fasting periods, and especially in anticipation of the beginning or end of a fasting period, meat and animal products are heavily and enthusiastically consumed.

Unlike all other African countries, Ethiopia claims to have never been colonized, although the Italians did "visit" a few times during the last century and put in a mighty good effort. That influence can still be seen in popular pasta dishes and spicy marinara sauces, but for the most part, Ethiopian cuisine has long been left unchanged.

The Ingredients

While the bulk of the ingredients needed for these recipes really are a snap to locate, there are a few that are a little more difficult to find. I know that for many people, tracking down exotic ingredients can be an enjoyable scavenger hunt and a part of cooking fun. But for those who don't enjoy this challenge, I've tried to make the most obscure ingredients optional whenever possible without compromising flavor.

If you're not sure where to find Ethiopian specialty ingredients in your area, check online. (See the resources listed on page 179.) You can also contact local Ethiopian restaurants, as some might be willing to sell ingredients to you directly or can point you toward local suppliers. Most large cities have Indian grocery stores, which can be good sources for many of the spices you'll need. Lucky you if you have an Ethiopian market in your city!

On page 19 you'll find a brief list that covers many of the ingredients you'll want to have on hand to make these recipes. The list can also help you translate Amharic ingredients you might find while shopping, since they're often not in English. (Amharic is Ethiopia's official language.)

Below is a list of what I keep in my pantry so I can whip up the flavors of old Abyssinia on a whim. Items that are more common and familiar are listed as "The Basics," without any discussion about them, but for more specialized products, I've included explanations to help you track down the right thing. To keep quality high and costs low, I recommend purchasing organic products in bulk whenever possible.

SPICES AND HERBS

Store all dried spices and herbs in tightly sealed containers away from direct heat, moisture, and sunlight. Avoid purchasing any spices and herbs in jars that look old and dusty (unless you plan on selling them as vintage cooking accoutrements in your Etsy shop).

The Basics: Ground allspice, whole black peppercorns, cayenne, ground cinnamon, whole cloves, coriander seeds, cumin seeds, fresh gingerroot, granulated onion, and ground turmeric.

Ajwain: This small seed goes by lots of names, including bishop's weed, carom seed, and *netch azmud* (in Ethiopian stores), but I think it's known best by its

Hindi name, *ajwain*. While not spicy, it has a strong, hard-to-describe, earthy flavor. Look for it in Indian grocery stores.

Basil: Any variety of dried basil will do. For recipes that call for chopped fresh basil, I use Italian basil leaves.

Cardamom, green: Green cardamom seeds are small yet strongly flavored, with a slight menthol flavor. Although they can be purchased whole in jars or in bulk, the seeds are the most flavorful when purchased in the pod. Just remove the seeds from the pod by lightly hitting the pod with the bottom of a jar. For ground cardamom, I maximize flavor and minimize effort (cardamom seeds are hard and therefore difficult to grind by hand) by using my trusty electric spice grinder.

Fenugreek seeds: Fenugreek seeds are golden, with a slightly bitter bite. They go by all sorts of names: in Indian groceries look for *methi*, and in Ethiopian markets, *abish*. Like cardamom, fenugreek can be tricky to grind by hand, so I use an electric spice grinder for them as well.

Garlic: The recipes in this book call for two forms of garlic: raw cloves and granulated. I peel the fresh cloves by giving them a hard smash with the bottom of a can or glass jar (the papery skin will come right off). Then I use a metal garlic press, which yields about one teaspoon of pressed garlic from two medium cloves. I don't recommend mincing garlic by hand for two reasons: First, these recipes call for so much garlic that if you minced it by hand it would take forever and ever. Second, garlic flavor is stronger and more pungent when the cloves are pressed or grated; the same intensity can't be had with hand mincing.

Horseradish, prepared: Most supermarkets carry prepared horseradish (grated horseradish root that's preserved in vinegar) in small jars in the refrigerator case, usually near the kosher pickles and sauerkraut. Look over the ingredients before you purchase prepared horseradish, as some brands contain dairy products. Prepared horseradish has a delicious, zesty bite and is a great addition to dressings and sauces (add it to ketchup for a superfast cocktail sauce).

New Mexico chile powder: New Mexico chile powder is a dark spice made from dried and ground reddish-brown chiles. While somewhat spicy, the powder is packed with flavor and is considerably milder than cayenne or jalapeño chiles. Look for the ground chile powder in Latin grocery stores. Alternatively, purchase bags of New Mexico chiles whole, from well-stocked supermarkets, and grind them yourself. For more information on grinding your own chile powder, see *Berbere* Paste (page 22).

Nigella: Nigella, also called *nigella sativa* or black cumin, is a dark, round seed that's used as a spice in many culinary traditions, including Ethiopian and Indian cuisines. It can be purchased whole or ground, but because it goes by different names, it can be a little tricky to locate. It's easiest to find nigella in Ethiopian grocery stores under its Amharic names, *tikur azmud* and *tikur qimem*, or in Indian grocery stores under its Hindi name, *kalonji*. Be careful purchasing nigella in Indian markets, though, because it's often confused with a different seed called *kala jeera* (which is shaped more like a caraway seed), as that's also commonly referred to as black cumin.

Nutmeg: I think nutmeg tastes best when the whole seed is freshly grated at home using a handheld fine grater (such as a Microplane). It's a snap to do, and whole nutmeg can be stored for a long time without diminished vibrancy.

Paprika: Paprika is a bright-red powder made from ground ripe peppers. It comes in many varieties, including hot, mild, and smoked. Choose a mild, non-smoked paprika with no heat for these recipes.

Salt: All of the recipes in this book were tested using fine iodized sea salt.

LEGUMES

The broad category of legumes includes dried beans, split peas, and lentils. Legumes are easy to find, inexpensive, nutritious, and keep for months. Store them in tightly sealed containers in the pantry or freezer. For tips on cleaning and cooking legumes, see page 15.

Chickpeas: The beloved and humble chickpea goes by a variety of names, but the most common are garbanzo bean and *chana*. Chickpeas are easy to find either dried or canned. I prefer the creamy texture of home-cooked chickpeas (I cook mine in a slow cooker overnight while I sleep), but I also always keep a few cans in the pantry for hummus emergencies.

Fava beans: Commonly known as broad beans, fava beans come in several varieties; the easiest to locate are the large greenish-white beans. This popular variety is readily available in Latin, European, and Mediterranean markets, but it's not the one you want to buy for these recipes. Instead, head to your local Middle Eastern market and keep your eyes peeled for small, roundish favas, also known as bell or marrone peas. You'll be able to find them dried or canned, although I find the canned beans are generally a bit mealy. See *Shehan Ful* (page 46) and the resources (page 179) for more info.

Lentils, brown and green: Brown and green lentils are what I call "supermarket lentils." They are inexpensive and easy to find in almost any grocery store. I try to keep at least one pound of dried green or brown lentils in the pantry at all times.

Lentils, du Puy: Also known as French lentils, the petite du Puy lentils hold their shape well after being cooked, making them ideal to use in salads. Although a little harder to locate than their more common counterparts, dried du Puy lentils can usually be found in Mediterranean or European specialty stores, natural food stores, and well-stocked supermarkets. If you can't be bothered to track them down, sturdy supermarket lentils make a fine replacement.

Lentils, red: Known in Hindi as *masoor dal*, red lentils are small, salmon-colored lentils that cook quickly into a pale-yellow purée. They're super easy to find in well-stocked supermarkets, natural food stores, and Middle Eastern, Mediterranean, Indian, and Ethiopian markets.

Soy milk: The recipes in this book were developed using Westsoy organic unsweetened plain soy milk. It's a full-fat soy milk containing only soybeans and water. If you prefer, other unsweetened nondairy milks can be substituted in the recipes, except for *Ayib* (page 36), which requires this specific type of soy milk.

Split peas: Nothing compares to the creaminess of split peas. In Ethiopian restaurants, you'll almost always be served a dish containing yellow split peas, but if you want a little variety, green split peas work just as well. When shopping in Indian markets, be careful not to confuse yellow split peas with their doppelganger *chana dal*, since they're actually different legumes.

Tempeh: Tempeh is a fermented food made from whole, cultured soybeans. It has a firm, meaty texture and an earthy, mushroomesque flavor. Tempeh should never be eaten raw, and it benefits from a quick steam (see page 144), which tenderizes it and removes any bitterness.

Textured soy protein: Textured soy protein, called TSP for short, is a dry, defatted soy product that resembles the texture of ground meat when it's hydrated in hot liquid. Since many brands of TSP are processed using hexane or other chemicals, I avoid that junk by purchasing organic TSP, which is also GMO-free. It's available via Bob's Red Mill (see page 179).

Tofu: Look for the firmest tofu you can find. If it seems wobbly and wet when you unpackage it, give it a good pressing. If you've never pressed tofu before, all you need to do is wrap it in a clean, dry tea towel, put it on a rimmed baking sheet or in a small baking pan, and balance something heavy on top, such as books or a piece of heavy cookware, and let it rest for about thirty minutes. Drain off the liquid and the tofu will be ready to use.

White beans: There are numerous varieties of white beans, and they're probably all dee-licious. Any small, creamy, white bean will do in these recipes. I use great Northern beans and white kidney beans, also known as cannellini beans.

FLOURS, GRAINS, AND STARCHES

The Basics: Cornstarch.

Chickpea flour: Chickpea flour is one of my favorite pantry staples, although in its raw state it tastes like absolute hell (trust me, don't taste it uncooked). It goes by many names, including garbanzo bean flour and *besan* or *gram* flour in Indian markets (where it's super cheap and easy to find). I store mine tightly wrapped in the freezer, where it stays fresh for ages.

Corn grits: Made from pulverized corn, corn grits are cooked with water to make a breakfast porridge that's especially popular in the southern United States. While some folks like to debate the issue, I find dry polenta and corn grits interchangeable. If you have the option between white and yellow grits, scoop up the yellow ones, since they're my favorite.

Oat flour: Oat flour can usually be found in shops that are well stocked with gluten-free products, but it's also easy to make oat flour at home. All you need is a blender or spice grinder (see page 13). I keep gluten-free rolled oats in my freezer to grind into flour on an as-needed basis.

Potato starch: Not to be confused with potato flour, which is made from pulverized potatoes, potato starch is extracted from potatoes. I use it as a binder in baking to lighten heavy flour and to give baked savory foods a crunchy coating. Look for it in the gluten-free or bulk aisle of supermarkets or natural food stores or in East Asian supermarkets.

Sorghum flour: Sorghum flour is one of my favorite flours to cook and bake with. Compared with stronger-tasting gluten-free flours, it has a light, neutral flavor. Bob's Red Mill (see page 179) packages white sorghum flour, which is often available at supermarkets and natural food stores in the gluten-free section, or look for it at Indian markets under its Hindi name *jowar*, or in Ethiopian markets.

Tapioca starch: Tapioca starch is also known as tapioca flour. Tapioca comes from the cassava root (the same root as yuca). Tapioca starch is great for binding, lightening heavy flours, and creating chewy textures in baked goods. You can find it readily and inexpensively in East Asian grocery stores and in packages in the gluten-free baking section of well-stocked supermarkets. Look for tapioca starch at Bob's Red Mill (see page 179).

Teff flour: Teff is a very tiny grain (some say it's the smallest known grain) native to Ethiopia. It's milled to make teff flour. Despite its small size, teff is a powerhouse of nutrition: it's rich in iron, calcium, protein, and fiber. Like many grains, teff comes in several varieties and colors, including white or ivory, brown, and red. However, I haven't noticed any significant difference in taste; the difference is mostly visual. When purchasing teff flour, double-check the package to make sure it actually contains the flour and not whole teff; it's easy to mix them up since the grain is so small.

Vital wheat gluten: Gluten is a protein found in wheat, barley, and rye. Vital wheat gluten is the powdered form of this protein. Vital wheat gluten adds stability and stretch to dough and can be used to quickly and easily make seitan and other kinds of vegan meats.

BAKING SUPPLIES AND OTHER PANTRY ITEMS

The Basics: Agave nectar, baking powder, baking soda, candied ginger, cream of tartar, pure vanilla extract, and unsalted tomato paste.

Instant yeast: Instant yeast can be found in the baking aisle of almost any supermarket. It comes in packets, just like regular baking yeast. Look for it under the brand name Rapid Rise by Fleischmann's.

Lasagna noodles: Feel free to use whatever variety of lasagna noodles you fancy. I usually buy the Tinkyada brand, since it's whole grain (brown rice), gluten-free, and just as tasty as its wheat-based counterpart.

Nutritional yeast flakes: Nutritional yeast flakes and I have had a long, shameless love affair. I use the flakes in recipes for their umami flavor and to add a savory, cheesy bite. Like any self-respecting vegan, I only buy the kind fortified with vitamin B_{12}, and I usually find it in the bulk-foods section of natural food stores or well-stocked markets. You can also sometimes find it packaged in canisters and bags in the grocery or supplement aisle. If you're concerned about eating live yeast, don't worry; nutritional yeast isn't active. It's also gluten-free.

Rice paper: Rice paper, or *banh trang* in Vietnamese, refers to the very thin, translucent, dried sheets typically used as wrappers. Because they are dried, they must be briefly softened in water before using so they become pliable. I use them to wrap all sorts of morsels; they also can serve as quick crusts for gluten-free baked treats. You can find rice paper in the international section of well-stocked supermarkets; they're also available in every shape and size at East Asian markets.

Table wine: Almost any kind of red or white table wine will work in these recipes, as long as you stay away from those that are overly sweet. I recommend buying one you'd be happy to drink, since the recipes that call for wine don't use that much of it.

Unbleached granulated sugar: Unbleached granulated sugar is cream- or caramel-colored sugar that can be used just like its white counterpart; the main difference is that it hasn't been bleached. Look for it in the bulk bins or in packages in well-stocked supermarkets and natural food stores.

Vegan cheese: While there's only one recipe in this book that calls for vegan cheese, it's important to note that whichever brand you choose, it should melt easily.

ETHIOPIAN SPECIALTY INGREDIENTS

Berbere: A spicy red spice blend, *berbere* (see page 21) is a mainstay of Ethiopian *kay wot* (see page 68).

Injera: A staple food in Ethiopia, *injera* is a fermented sourdough pancake, commonly made from teff flour and sometimes other grains, such as wheat, barley, or rice (see pages 26 and 28).

Koseret: *Koseret,* or *kosearut,* is a dried, strongly scented, twiggy herb that's easy to find if you have access to an Ethiopian market. Otherwise, bribe a friend from a big city to send you some, order it from an online supplier, or just leave it out.

Mitmita: A fiery-hot Ethiopian spice blend used as a condiment, *mitmita* (see page 39) is usually made from bird's eye chiles, cardamom, cloves, and salt.

Shiro powder: *Shiro* powder (see page 107), a staple protein source in Ethiopia, is a finely ground spiced powder made from cooked and dried legumes. It's made into a thin, gravy-like sauce with the addition of oil and water. Look for packaged *shiro* powder on the shelves of Ethiopian grocery stores or via online specialty markets. Spicy *shiro* powder is sold as *miten or kay shiro,* and lightly seasoned *shiro* powder as white or *nech shiro.*

Teff flour: See Flours, Grains, and Starches (page 9).

NUTS, SEEDS, AND OILS

I recommend storing oils at room temperature, away from direct sunlight, and storing seeds and nuts in bags and glass jars in the freezer (they don't need to be defrosted before using).

The Basics: Extra-virgin olive oil, organic canola oil, roasted peanuts, sesame seeds, and raw sunflower seeds.

Cashews: Look for creamy white, unroasted, unsalted cashew pieces for the recipes in this book (they're much less costly than whole nuts).

Coconut oil: Coconut oil is one of my favorite oils to use in the kitchen; it has a high smoke point and tastes great. I use two types of coconut oil in these recipes: refined, which has a neutral flavor, and unrefined, or virgin, which has a pronounced coconut flavor. Coconut oil can be a little challenging to deal with in cold weather, since it becomes solid at temperatures below 76 degrees F.

Flaxseeds: Flaxseeds are commonly available in two varieties: golden and dark brown. In this book, in recipes for baked goods that use ground flaxseeds are used as a binder, either type will do. For traditional Ethiopian recipes, the dark brown seeds are specified.

Peanut butter: Look for natural unsweetened peanut butter made with only peanuts.

FRUITS AND VEGGIES

The Basics: Beets, blueberries, butternut squash, cabbage, carrots, cauliflower, collard greens, eggplants, green beans, green onions, hot chiles, kale, lemons, limes, mushrooms, okra, onions, potatoes, romaine lettuce, spinach, sweet potatoes, and tomatoes.

Kitchen Tools and Equipment

Feel an Ethiopian cooking spree coming on? Here's a list of equipment that will help you crank out Ethiopian yummies faster and easier than you can scream *beyaynetu* ten times fast.

Blender: You don't need a fancy blender for any of the recipes in this book, but if you have an immersion or stick blender, it will be particularly handy for blending *Shiro* (page 108) and making *Ersho* (batter for *Injera*, page 28).

Colander: Large metal and plastic colanders are useful for draining lentils, split peas, and pasta.

Electric spice grinder or coffee grinder: I have a coffee grinder that's dedicated to pulverizing spices and seeds and for making flour. In addition to a few sharp knives, it's one of the few tools in my kitchen I wouldn't want to do without.

Fine-mesh sieve: A medium-sized sieve with a fine metal mesh is what I recommend for the cheese and seed milk recipes.

Food processor: Any size food processor, even a mini chopper, is especially helpful for chopping onions, grinding toasted seeds, blending, and puréeing tofu.

Garlic press: A metal garlic press is the fastest and most efficient tool for working through a head of garlic cloves lickety-split.

Microplane: I recommend Microplane brand graters to make grating ginger a super-easy task.

Nonreactive bowls: Glass, plastic, ceramic, and enamel are nonreactive, which means they don't react to acidic ingredients. Nonreactive bowls are recommended for making *Ersho* (page 28).

Parchment paper: Parchment paper is used to quickly give any baking pan or baking sheet a nonstick surface. Parchment paper can be found at any well-stocked grocery store and comes bleached or unbleached. Don't confuse parchment paper with waxed paper, which will burn and melt at high temperatures.

Round platters and trays: I have several large enameled platters that I use for Ethiopian smorgasbords (see Cooking for a Crowd, page 17). If you don't already own some, purchase a few beautiful platters and trays so you can serve these recipes in style.

Techniques, Time-Savers, and Tips

TECHNIQUES

ere are some helpful techniques and shortcuts I frequently use when I'm cooking Ethiopian food.

Baking Sweet Potatoes

Preheat the oven to 400 degrees F. Line a baking sheet with parchment paper. Pierce each sweet potato several times with the tines of a fork and put on the prepared baking sheet. Bake for 45 minutes to 1½ hours (depending on the size and thickness of the sweet potatoes), until tender, turning the potatoes over halfway through the cooking process.

Grinding Oat Flour

Oat flour is easy to find in stores, but it's even easier and less expensive to make at home if you have an electric spice grinder and rolled oats. Fill the spice grinder with oats and grind until fine. That's it! If you have a high-powered blender, that'll work, too.

Boiling and Peeling Potatoes

Fill a large pot with salted water and add the potatoes. Bring to a boil over high heat. Decrease the heat and simmer until the potatoes are fork-tender but not mushy, 20 to 30 minutes (depending on the size and thickness of the potatoes). Drain the potatoes and rinse them under cold water until cool enough to handle; the skins should peel off easily using your fingers.

Cutting Carrot Sticks

Peel each carrot and cut it into 1¾-inch lengths. Cut the thinner lengths into quarters and the thicker pieces into fifths or sixths.

Cooking Dried Beans

Put 1 cup of dried beans in a large bowl with 7 cups of water. Cover and refrigerate for 8 to 10 hours. Drain the beans and discard the soaking water. Transfer the beans to a medium pot and cover with 7 cups of fresh water. Bring to a boil over high heat. Decrease the heat to medium and simmer, stirring occasionally, until the beans are very tender and soft. This can take from 45 minutes to several hours depending on the type of bean. Drain the beans, reserving the cooking liquid if it's used in the recipe. Use the beans immediately or store them in a covered container in the fridge for up to 3 days. Rinse and drain stored beans before using.

Peeling Fresh Ginger

I find the easiest way to peel fresh ginger is with a teaspoon. Turn the spoon so it's facing down and use the curved edge at the top and sides to scrape the ginger firmly. The skin will come right off.

Peeling Tomatoes

If you're like me and don't appreciate the way a tomato's skin peels off during cooking, here's an easy method for removing the skins before you cook the tomatoes. Fill a medium pot with water and bring to a boil over high heat. Turn each tomato over and score a small X on its bottom, just through the skin of the fruit. Submerge the tomato in the boiling water for 30 seconds. Quickly remove the tomato with a slotted spoon and plunge it into a bowl of cold water or ice water. Voila! The skin will slide right off.

Roasting Beets

Preheat the oven to 425 degrees F. Scrub the beets well, cut off any long tails, and wrap each beet tightly in aluminum foil. Put the beets on a baking sheet or in a baking pan and bake for 55 to 75 minutes (smaller beets will cook faster), until very tender, turning each beet over every 15 minutes to prevent scorching. Let the beets rest at room temperature until they're cool enough to handle, then open each packet and peel under cold running water. Cut off the coarse stem end from each beet and the skin should slip off easily with a little rubbing from your fingers.

Toasting and Grinding Flaxseeds

Put the flaxseeds in a medium skillet and cook over medium-high heat, stirring almost constantly to prevent burning. As soon as the seeds begin to pop, cover the pan and shake it continuously (don't scratch your stove top!), putting it on and off the heat as needed, until the seeds are toasted and fragrant, about 2 minutes from the first pop (just like stove-top popcorn). Immediately remove the pan from the heat and transfer the seeds to a ceramic plate to cool. When the seeds are completely cool, put them in a clean electric coffee or spice grinder and grind them into a fine powder.

Washing and Cutting Dark Leafy Greens

Collards and other hearty greens can be gritty if they aren't washed well. The best way to clean them is to cut out and discard the large center rib from each leaf. Then fill the kitchen sink with water and swish the greens around. Let the greens soak for a few minutes to loosen any dirt, which will sink to the bottom. Pick up the leaves carefully so you don't redistribute the dirt and rinse each leaf individually under running water.

To cut the greens (remember, the thick center rib from each leaf has already been removed), stack four or five leaves on a cutting board and roll them together lengthwise (side to side) into a tight log. Cut the log into ribbons about one-quarter inch wide, and then cut through the ribbons to dice. Repeat with the remaining leaves.

TIME-SAVERS

I'm more of a messy cook than a *mise en place* cook, but when it comes to preparing multiple Ethiopian dishes, I've learned that being organized and planning ahead can help the process go a whole lot faster and smoother and keep the cook from getting stressed out. Here are a few suggestions:

General Tips

- A food processor or mini chopper can make the tearful task of mincing countless cups of onion an easy job. Simply pulse a mess of onions, throw 'em into a large bowl, scoop into your stash with a measuring cup as you cook, and be on your happy way. Keep in mind that 1 cup of hand-minced onion is equivalent to ¾ cup of onion minced in a food processor, so use a little less than the recipe calls for if you use this no-tears method.
- Make *Ye'qimem Zeyet* (page 25) and *Berbere* Paste (page 22) the week before your feast.
- Before you start cooking, press an entire head of garlic into a small cup or bowl and measure as needed.
- Before you start cooking, peel (see page 14) and grate fresh ginger.

Legume Prep and Cooking

The term "legumes" covers the broad category of lentils, split peas, and beans. Since many of the *wot* recipes in the book are based on lentils or split peas, I thought it would be a good idea to share some helpful tips about preparing them.

- Cook legumes up to three days before a feast. Drain and reserve the cooking liquid. Store the legumes and their cooking liquid separately in tightly covered containers in the fridge.
- Legumes, especially those sold in bulk, are generally dusty and may contain small pebbles or debris. Just before cooking them, sort through the legumes carefully and remove any pebbles, dirt, or twigs. Then rinse and drain the legumes a few times until the water runs clear.

- Legumes, especially lentils and split peas, tend to create a lot of foam (which should be skimmed off with a slotted spoon) as they're coming to a boil. If you're not paying close attention, the pot could easily spill over. If that happens, just clean up the mess as best you can and add some additional water to the pot so the legumes don't scorch.

- Try to serve more than one kind of legume-based dish, as variety is always welcome on an Ethiopian platter.

TIPS

Wot's Cookin'

Wot is the general term used to describe any of the primary dishes in this magical, delicious cuisine. *Wot* vary in texture from a thin gravy to a thick, sauce-laden stew. Their color ranges from deep, dark reds to light yellows. And their spiciness runs the gamut from so mild it wouldn't make a baby cry to hella-hella hot. The main thing all *wot* have in common is that they're mopped up and eaten with *injera*.

Wot generally fall into two categories: *Kay wot* are spicy sauces and stews characterized by their red (*kay*) color, which comes from *berbere* (see page 21). And milder *alicha wot*, which as a rule don't contain *berbere*, can still be spicy depending on how much hot green chile they contain.

The wot in this book have been organized into three chapters: *kay wot*, *alicha wot*, and *shiro*. If a dish is described simply as *wot*, assume it's a *kay wot*, as stews that don't contain *berbere* are usually referred to as *alicha*.

Mixin' It Up

Usually I'm a bit of a traditionalist when it comes to cooking, but there's something about the flavors of Ethiopian food that make me want to add little bits of it to everything I cook. If you're craving the flavors but aren't up for cooking a huge Ethiopian bash, the easiest way to get what you're after is with *berbere* (see page 21) or *Ye'qimem Zeyet* (page 25). I've used these seasonings in several fusion-style recipes, including Ethiopian-Style Mac 'n' Cheesie (page 126), Garlic Jojos (page 128), and Ethiopian-Style Roasted Brussels Sprouts (page 125). Here are a couple more ideas:

- Try *berbere* in chili, taco filling, frijoles, tamale dough or filling, mayo, guacamole, pizza sauce, or soft pretzels (brush them with *Ye'qimem Zeyet* and dip them in *Senafich*, page 44).

- Try *Ye'qimem Zeyet* (page 25) sprinkled on popcorn, garlic bread, baked potatoes, roasted vegetables, mashed potatoes, pasta, and corn on the cob.

Cooking for a Crowd

One of my favorite things about eating Ethiopian food is having a meal with lots of varied dishes to taste and enjoy. The problem is, if I'm cooking at home just for me and Dazee, I end up with a huge amount of food. The best way I've found to resolve this dilemma is to make a party of it. Besides, cooking Ethiopian food is an easy way to feed lots of people, and because the food is eaten by hand from platters, it ultimately saves time afterward in the dirty-dish department.

A group of six hungry people can usually be fed well with three different dishes, as long as a big green salad is included and there's enough *injera* to go around. If you're cooking for a larger group, determine how much food to prepare by calculating how many platters of food you need to serve. In general, one large platter is enough to generously feed three or four people if there is a total of about six cups of a variety of food along with a large salad and plenty of *injera* for everyone. If you don't have enough serving platters to go around, more people sharing a platter is acceptable for a group of friendly folks. But be warned: if you crowd too many people around one platter, there's bound to be an ugly brawl over the Ethiopian-Style Mac 'n' Cheesie (page 126).

For a group of twenty guests, plan on making enough food to fill five platters. This adds up to one large bowl of salad and about thirty cups of food. Once you know how much you need, it's a snap to figure out what to make, since each recipe provides the yield in cups. The additional good news is that the legume recipes can easily be doubled or tripled, and a simple salad is a breeze to throw together. Plus, a few of the recipes are no fuss at all, since they can be baked in the oven with minimal supervision.

Here's a sample menu for a feast that's sure to garner the love and adoration of twenty of your favorite friends. It makes enough food to fill five platters with two big spoonfuls (about one cup) of each dish:

- A big bowl of leafy salad (page 132), large enough to divide among five platters.
- A double recipe of *Ye'misser Wot* (page 72) = 8 cups.
- A double recipe of *Ye'ater Kik Alicha* (page 96) = 7 cups.
- A double recipe of *Ye'tikil Gomen Be'karot* (page 123) = 8 cups.
- One recipe of Ethiopian-Style Mac 'n' Cheesie (page 126) = 9 cups.

When you're choosing a menu to prepare, it's important to go with a variety of colors, textures, and flavors. A good approach is to include a variety of taste and texture experiences: creamy, crunchy, mild, tangy, and spicy. Even if you're just cooking for yourself, incorporate as many contrasting flavors and textures as possible, since that's one of the most enjoyable aspects of eating this magical cuisine.

Once you've figured out what you're going to make, you'll need to plan how you'll serve all of these delicious morsels. I suggest investing in some large enameled platters. They're beautiful and relatively inexpensive and will make the dining experience more festive and the food easier to share and eat. I've found that most Ethiopian grocery stores have a supply of enameled platters, but I've also come upon them at large East Asian supermarkets. If you're willing to spend a bit more money, check out online sources, such as eBay and Etsy, for gorgeous vintage platters.

Here are six sure-fire ways to ensure success:

1. Set time aside and cook your tokus off. This includes time for planning, prep, and advance cooking, so you don't get stressed out trying to get everything done at the same time.

2. Move some furniture to clear out an eating area, and spread clean blankets or tablecloths on the floor.

3. Stock up on hand soap and pretty towels. Establish a no-shoe and no-sweaty-socks policy (so gross!) to keep the eating area clean.

4. Watch for dogs and other low-lying animals (a friend once brought her mini dachshund to one of our dinners, and the doggy proceeded to run happily across two full platters of food before anyone could catch up with her).

5. Eat from overflowing platters (remember, keep it to just three or four folks per tray).

6. Play Ethiopian music for an ultra-swanky themed event.

Ethiopian Grocery List

I f you're lucky enough to live near a well-stocked Ethiopian grocery store, you can take this handy shopping list with you. To help you easily identify items on the shelf, the words in parentheses are in Amharic, and items followed by an asterisk can also be found in many Indian markets and some well-stocked supermarkets.

If you find something you're interested in buying and you're having trouble figuring out whether or not it's vegan, know that there's no word in Amharic for "vegetarian" or "vegan," unfortunately. However, you can ask if something is a fasting food (*ye'tshom megib*) or if it has any animal ingredients in it (*keensisat tewatsio wuchi yehone megib*). Generally, the breads (*dabo*) and crunchy snacks (*dabo kolo* or *kolo*) are good bets, but the fried stuffed pastries (*sambusas*) can be filled with meat or lentils, so be sure to double-check before you dig in.

SPICES

bishop's weed, *ajwain* (*nech azmud*)*	coriander (*dimbilal*)*	nigella seeds (*tikur azmud*)*
basil (*besobila*)*	cumin (*kimun*)*	turmeric (*ird*) or curry powder*
cardamom (*korerima*)*	fenugreek seeds (*abish*)*	whole nutmeg (*laylen*)
cinnamon (*kerefa*)*	lippia (*koseret*)	yellow mustard seeds (*senafich*)*
cloves (*krinfud*)*		

SPICE BLENDS

alicha qimem	*mitmita*	tea spice (*shai be'qimem*)
awaze (in jars)	spices for seasoned oil or butter (*ye'kibbeh manteria*)	*ye'wot qimem* or *tikur qimem*
berbere		

FLOURS

chickpea flour (*ye'shimbra duket*)*	*shiro* powder, mild (*nech shiro*)	sorghum flour (*ye'zenegada duket* or *ye'mashila duket*)*
oat flour (*ye'aja duket*)	*shiro* powder, spicy (*kay shiro*)	teff flour, ivory and brown (*ye'tef duket*)

PREPARED FOODS

bread (*ambasha* or *dabo*)	fried dough snacks (*dabo kolo*)	lentil *sambusas*
dried *injera* (*derkosh*)	*injera*	roasted snacks (*kolo*)

SEEDS

flaxseeds (*telba*)	sesame seeds (*selit*)	shelled raw sunflower seeds (*souf*)

LEGUMES

brown or green lentils (*diffen misser*)	fava beans (*bakela* or *ful*)	split peas (*ater* or *kik*)*
chickpeas (*shimbra*)*	red lentils (*misser*)*	

EQUIPMENT

large enameled platters	small woven stand or basket (*mesob*)	*injera* cooking pan (*mitad*)

In this chapter, you'll find recipes for what I consider the holy trinity of vegan Ethiopian cooking: *berbere, ye'qimem zeyet*, and *injera*. These recipes will lead you on your way to turning your kitchen into an Ethiopian *beyaynetu* factory.

the holy trinity

notes on berbere

Berbere is literally one of the yummiest spices I keep in my pantry. If you're already a fan of Ethiopian food, *berbere* is probably one of the flavors you ruminate on while daydreaming about your favorite veggie platter. In case you're unfamiliar with it, *berbere* is a spice blend made from moderately hot red peppers and a slew of other spices. It's best known for its use in spicy red sauces and stews called *kay wot* (see page 67). It can also be used to season all sorts of other kinds of food, from creamy salad dressings to pastry crusts. It's one of the most predominant and notable flavors in Ethiopian cooking, and it's worth making or seeking out (even if you have to special order it).

My favorite is ground *berbere* sold as a dry powder in containers in Ethiopian grocery stores or from online retailers. It's imported from Africa and contains an array of seasonings, including spices, chiles, and probably even special Ethiopian pixie dust that isn't readily available in the West. Imported *berbere* definitely packs some heat, but it contains a lot of other notable flavors too. I find domestic *berbere*, which is usually seasoned primarily with cayenne, to be too spicy and overpowering; the heat from the chiles shouldn't drown out the flavors of the other ingredients. When you're shopping for *berbere*, check the ingredients (and if possible, ask for a sample taste), and stay away from any that list cayenne as the primary or only chile.

For avid Ethiopian cooks, I recommend making your own *berbere* paste and also tracking down a few of the imported ground blends. *Berbere* varies from maker to maker, and the more variations you collect, the more interesting and unique your *kay wot* will taste. For more information on cooking with *berbere*, see the chapter on *kay wot* (pages 67 to 92).

his recipe produces a *berbere* paste rather than a ground powder and uses moderately hot New Mexico chiles and a little bit of cayenne for heat. If you're a fan of milder flavors, start with a small amount of cayenne and increase it if desired. I find that one and a half teaspoons will make a

berbere paste

A SPICY RED-CHILE SEASONING BLEND

MAKES ¾ CUP

- 2 tablespoons **organic canola oil**
- ⅓ cup **minced onion**
- 6 cloves **garlic, pressed or grated** (1 tablespoon)
- 2 teaspoons **peeled and grated fresh ginger**
- ¾ teaspoon **salt**
- 1 tablespoon **whole coriander seeds**
- 8 **whole cloves**
- ½ teaspoon **whole nigella seeds** (optional)
- ¼ teaspoon **whole *ajwain* seeds** (optional)
- ¼ teaspoon **whole fenugreek seeds**
- ¼ teaspoon **husked green cardamom seeds**
- ¼ cup **New Mexico chile powder** (see sidebar, page 23)
- 2 tablespoons **granulated onion**
- 1 tablespoon **mild paprika**
- ½ teaspoon **cayenne,** plus more if desired
- ¼ teaspoon **ground cinnamon**
- 8 large **fresh basil leaves**
- ½ cup **water**

Put 1 tablespoon of the oil and the minced onion, garlic, ginger, and salt in a small saucepan. Cook over medium-high heat, stirring frequently to keep the garlic from burning, until the onion is soft and golden brown, about 5 minutes. Transfer to a blender or mini food processor.

Put the remaining tablespoon of oil and the coriander, cloves, optional nigella, optional *ajwain*, fenugreek, and cardamom in the same saucepan and cook over medium heat, stirring frequently, until fragrant, about 2 minutes. Quickly add the chile powder, granulated onion, paprika, cayenne, and cinnamon and cook, stirring constantly, for 1 minute longer. Transfer to the blender and add the basil and water. Process into a thick, smooth paste. Taste and add up to 2 tablespoons additional cayenne, ½ teaspoon at a time, if desired.

Per tablespoon: 39 calories, 1 g protein, 2 g fat (0 g sat), 4 g carbohydrates, 112 mg sodium, 10 mg calcium, 1 g fiber

---

Using *Berbere* Paste

Berbere Paste produces *kay wot* dishes that are lighter in color than those that contain ground imported *berbere,* but they're full of flavor. Please refer to the *kay wot* section (see page 67) for more info about how to use this important Ethiopian ingredient.

moderately hot paste that's similar to the heat of imported ground *berbere*. Be careful when adding more than one teaspoon of cayenne, since the *kay wot* recipes generally call for several tablespoons at a time. And of course, if you're sensitive to spice and strong aromas, please ventilate the kitchen when you make this!

New Mexico Chile Powder

Stem, seed, and vein 1½ ounces of dried New Mexico chiles. Grind the chiles in an electric coffee mill or spice grinder until powdered. Yield: ¼ cup.

COOKING TIP: *Berbere* Paste will be a snap to make if the spices are pre-measured and organized into two small bowls before you begin cooking.

STORAGE TIP: Store *Berbere* Paste in a clean glass jar in the fridge for up to 3 weeks. Use a small spoon to tamp it down to get rid of air pockets and smooth the top. Clean the outer and inner lip of the jar with a clean, dry towel or cloth and add just enough neutral-tasting oil to completely cover the surface with a thin film. *Berbere* Paste may also be stored in the freezer. Simply freeze the whole jar or freeze tablespoons of the paste on a baking sheet and then transfer them to a ziplock freezer bag.

ye'qimem zeyet

notes on ye'qimem zeyet

Ye'qimem zeyet is the vegan version of *niter kibbeh* (seasoned clarified butter), which is among the most prominent ingredients and flavors in Ethiopian cooking. Because millions of orthodox Christians in Ethiopia eschew animal-based foods during their religious fasting periods, butter is generally reserved for meat and dairy dishes and oil for vegetable- and legume-based dishes (that's why there's typically so many vegan options at Ethiopian restaurants).

To make *ye'qimem zeyet*, vegetable oil is infused with a litany of spices and savory ingredients and the outcome adds a distinct pop of delectable Ethiopian joy to whatever it touches (including popcorn and mashed potatoes—just sayin').

The recipes in this book have been tested with *ye'qimem zeyet* made from a variety of vegan oils and solid fats. While any neutral-tasting oil will work well, I've found the combination of 75 percent oil and 25 percent solid fat to produce the best results. My preference is 1½ cups of organic canola oil and ½ cup of melted refined coconut oil (unrefined coconut oil tastes too coconutty for these recipes). This combination works great over high heat, has a texture reminiscent of clarified butter, and softens quickly at room temperature. Using only oil also works well, but I don't recommend using only solid fat; it gets too hard in the fridge, takes too long to soften, and is too difficult to spoon out and measure.

his recipe is quite flexible. Please don't skip it if you can't find some of the ingredients; instead, just omit what you can't find and include what you can. This recipe fills most of a pint jar, and keeping this flavorful oil on hand makes it easy to whip up Ethiopian food whenever your heart desires. I'm confident that once you taste it, you'll want extra in the fridge for spontaneous Ethiopian-themed slumber parties.

ye'qimem zeyet

SEASONED OIL

- 2 cups **neutral-tasting oil, melted refined coconut oil, melted vegan butter, or a combination**
- ⅓ cup **minced red onion or shallots**
- 12 cloves **garlic, pressed or grated** (2 tablespoons)
- 1 tablespoon **crumbled dried *koseret*** (optional; see page 10)
- 1 tablespoon **peeled and grated fresh ginger**
- ½ teaspoon **whole *ajwain* seeds** (optional; see page 4)
- ½ teaspoon **ground cardamom**
- ½ teaspoon **ground cinnamon**
- ½ teaspoon **whole fenugreek seeds**
- ½ teaspoon **ground turmeric**
- ½ teaspoon **whole nigella seeds** (optional; see page 6)
- 6 **fresh basil leaves**
- 6 **whole cloves**
- ¼ teaspoon **dried basil**
- ⅛ teaspoon **freshly grated nutmeg**

Combine all the ingredients in a medium saucepan. Bring to a simmer over medium heat, then decrease the heat to low (the oil should barely bubble) and cook, stirring occasionally, until the onion is soft and translucent and the oil is fragrant, about 15 minutes.

Let cool until the oil reaches room temperature. Strain through a fine-mesh sieve or double layer of cheesecloth, pressing out as much oil as possible from the solids before discarding them. Transfer to a clean glass jar and store in the refrigerator. Bring to room temperature and stir before using.

Per tablespoon: 169 calories, 0 g protein, 19 g fat (1 g sat), 1 g carbohydrates, 0 mg sodium, 4 mg calcium, 0 g fiber

STORAGE TIP: Strained and covered, *Ye'qimem Zeyet* can be stored in the fridge for up to 3 weeks or in the freezer for up to 2 months. If you use a solid fat (such as coconut oil or vegan butter), freeze the *Ye'qimem Zeyet* in ice-cube trays and then transfer the frozen cubes to a ziplock freezer bag.

notes on *injera* (AKA TEFF LOVE)

njera, the fermented sourdough crepe that's eaten with most Ethiopian food (some folks say it makes up the bulk of the Ethiopian diet) can be made from all sorts of milled grains, including barley, corn, rice, millet, sorghum, and wheat. However, it's most commonly made from teff.

If you're not familiar with teff, it's a teeny tiny grain that's a powerhouse of nutrition. Despite its diminutive size, teff packs a lot of protein, calcium, fiber, and iron. It's also gluten-free, a boon for gluten-intolerant folks like me. It comes in several colors, including white or ivory, red, and dark brown. It tastes great and is the grain I reach for when I want to add a whole-wheat vibe (without the wheat) to baked goods.

Teff is native to Ethiopia, and that's where you used to have to go to get it. However, over the last several years, teff has gained popularity in the West, in part because of the attention heirloom and ancient grains have received, and also because of a growing interest in gluten-free diets. Several farms in the United States have started growing teff, and they seem to be the main domestic suppliers nowadays (even the teff flour I buy at the Ethiopian store down the street comes from one of these farms).

I hope I don't shatter hearts when I tell you that most commercial *injera* in North America is rarely made from pure teff flour and thus is usually not gluten-free. Since teff is quite expensive, teff *injera* is commonly made with the addition of other grains, such as wheat or barley flours, to keep the cost down. Fortunately, I've noticed an increasing number of restaurants beginning to offer pure teff *injera* for an extra charge, though some might require twenty-four hour's notice. With the rising popularity of gluten-free diets, my hope is that this trend will grow.

Top: **Ye'tef Injera,** *page 26; bottom:* **Tempeh Salad,** *page 144*

Clockwise from top: **Shahan Ful,** *page 46;* **Ye'mashila Genfo,** *page 53;*
Ye'tofu Enkulal Firfir, *page 48;* **Ye'beqolo Genfo,** *page 52*

However, if gluten makes you sick, be aware that restaurants often purchase *injera* from wholesalers and may not realize their *injera* contains anything other than teff, or they may not know that barley and wheat contain gluten. So be a careful consumer and ask the right questions before you dig in.

I make my own 100 percent teff *injera* at home. In addition to it being wonderfully gluten-free, it has great flavor and the perfect amount of tang, which offers a good counterbalance to hot spices and heavy stews and sauces. Making *injera* at home takes a little finagling and time, but once you figure it out, you'll be storing jars of *ersho* (teff sourdough starter) in the back of your fridge like a champ. To get started, you'll need to stock up on teff flour (see page 9) and spend a few days fermenting a sourdough starter.

pparently, teff is the only grain to have a symbiotic relationship with yeast, which makes sense since, traditionally, teff starter is made with only teff flour and water. However, I've found this starter works best when I add active yeast. I've read that symbiotic yeast only flourishes on freshly ground teff flour, and that may be why the addition of active yeast is a necessary boost.

ersho

TEFF SOURDOUGH STARTER

MAKES 1¼ CUPS

1½ cups **teff flour, any variety**

1¼ cups **filtered water,** plus more if needed

2 teaspoons **instant yeast**

DAY 1. Combine 1 cup of the flour, 1 cup of the water, and the yeast in a large nonreactive bowl and whisk until smooth and well combined. Cover with a plate or clean, dry tea towel and put the bowl on a rimmed baking tray to catch any overflow (the mixture will bubble, rise, and fall). Let it rest undisturbed in a warm, draft-free place for 24 hours. In cooler months, you can put it in an unheated oven or on top of the fridge.

DAY 2. If any liquid has accumulated on the surface, carefully pour it off (it's okay if it's dark). Gently stir the bubbly mixture, incorporating any batter clinging to the sides of the bowl or plate. If you used a tea towel and it gets wet at any point, replace it with a dry one. Mix in ¼ cup of the flour and stir gently until smooth and well blended. Cover the bowl again and let it rest undisturbed in a warm, draft-free place for another 24 hours.

DAY 3. Before starting this step, read the troubleshooting tips that follow the recipe. In hot weather, skip this step and go directly to Day 4.

If any liquid has accumulated on the surface, carefully pour it off (it's okay if it's dark). Gently stir the bubbly mixture again, incorporating in any stray batter. Add the remaining ¼ cup of flour and the remaining ¼ cup of filtered water and stir gently to combine. If you've poured off any liquid, add a little bit more water; the starter should be the consistency of pancake batter. Cover again and let rest undisturbed in a warm, draft-free spot for 24 hours longer.

DAY 4. If any liquid has accumulated on the surface, carefully pour it off (it's okay if it's dark). Stir once more, gently incorporating any stray batter. Use immediately in *Ye'tef Injera* (page 30) or Cinnamon-Blueberry Sourdough Pancakes (page 54); this recipe yields enough for several batches of both.

Per 1¼ cups: 678 calories, 24 g protein, 6 g fat (0 g sat), 132 g carbohydrates, 30 mg sodium, 300 mg calcium, 24 g fiber

COOKING TIP: If you prefer to not have leftovers, feel free to halve the recipe.

TROUBLESHOOTING

- In hot weather, the starter has a tendency to over-ferment and may become too sour. To avoid this, skip Day 3 and move directly to the directions for Day 4 (you'll be decreasing the fermentation time by 24 hours and the flour by ¼ cup).

- Be sure that everything that comes in contact with the starter is clean, including all utensils, dishes, and especially your hands and fingernails; otherwise, you might introduce bacteria that could ruin the starter. There should never be any visible mold on the starter; if you see any, discard the batter and start over.

- Leftover starter can be kept in a clean, dry jar, loosely covered in the fridge. When you plan to use some of the starter, bring it to room temperature, feed it with equal amounts of teff flour and filtered water (I usually add 2 to 4 tablespoons of each), and let it rest in a warm spot for 24 hours. Stir the starter. If it's bubbly and active, proceed with the recipe; otherwise, toss it out and start over.

This recipe is for folks like me who don't own a *mitad* (a traditional *injera* griddle), as it produces *injera* that are smaller than those found in restaurants, making them more manageable to cook. If you've already made *Ersho* (page 28), homemade *injera* will take an additional thirty-six hours to ferment before they can be cooked.

ye'tef injera
TEFF SOURDOUGH CRÊPES

MAKES 16 (7-INCH) INJERA

3 cups **teff flour, any variety** (see cooking tip)

1 teaspoon **ground fenugreek**

5 tablespoons *Ersho* (page 28), **at room temperature**

4 cups **filtered water,** plus more if needed

½ teaspoon **salt**

DAY 1. Make the *injera* batter. Sift the flour and fenugreek into a large nonreactive bowl. Add the starter and water and whisk until smooth and well blended. Cover with a plate or clean, dry tea towel and let rest undisturbed in a warm, draft-free place for 24 hours. In cooler months, put it in an unheated oven or on top of the fridge.

DAY 2. If any liquid has accumulated on the surface, carefully pour it off (it's okay if it's dark). Gently stir the bubbly mixture, incorporating in any batter clinging to the sides of the bowl or plate. If you used a tea towel and it gets wet at any point, replace it with a dry one. Measure out ½ cup of the batter and transfer it to a small saucepan. Cook the batter over medium-high heat, stirring constantly, until the liquid evaporates and the batter turns into a thick, rubbery dough (once the pan gets hot, this will only take 2 to 3 minutes). Immediately remove from the heat and spread the dough out on a ceramic plate and let cool for 5 minutes. Return the cooked dough to the bowl of teff batter and blend using an immersion blender until smooth and bubbly. Alternatively, blend in batches using a food processor or blender and return the batter to the bowl. The batter should be the consistency of a thick slurry or crêpe batter; if it seems too thick, whisk in a little filtered water to thin it out. Cover with a clean, dry tea towel and let rest undisturbed in a warm, draft-free place for 24 hours. In cooler months, put it in an unheated oven or on top of the fridge. A few hours after blending, you should notice that the batter has risen and is actively bubbling.

DAY 3. If any dark liquid has accumulated on the surface, carefully pour it off (it's okay if it's dark). Add the salt and gently stir the bubbly *ersho* to combine; it should be the consistency of a thick slurry or thin crêpe batter. If it's too thick, add a small amount of filtered water as needed to thin.

To cook the *injera*, heat a nonstick flat griddle or skillet over medium heat. Line a counter or table with a large, clean, dry tea towel. Keep another dampened tea towel nearby.

Form the *injera* by pouring ⅓ cup of the batter into a disk on the hot griddle. Use the back of a small spoon to quickly and lightly smooth the batter into a 7-inch disk, starting in the center and working in concentric circles until you reach the edges (try to keep the center of the crêpe the thickest and the edges the thinnest). The disk should be about ¼ inch thick.

Cover the pan and cook the *injera* for 3 minutes (do not flip it, as *injera* are only cooked on one side). Fully cooked, the *injera* should be dry on the top with little holes that have formed over the entire surface; the bottom should be firm, smooth, and unbrowned. Depending on your cookware and stove, you'll most likely need to adjust the heat to achieve this. Use a flat, flexible spatula to loosen the *injera* and then quickly transfer it to the towel-lined surface. Cover it with another clean, dry tea towel.

Use the dampened towel to wipe off any visible starch on the pan or griddle. Repeat the cooking process until the batter is used up. As they cool, the *injera* will develop a spongy-stretchy texture, and they can be stacked without sticking.

Once they're completely cool, wrap them in a clean, dry tea towel and store them in a tightly closed ziplock bag. Be certain that the *injera* are dry; otherwise, the bag will collect moisture and the *injera* will spoil. If you notice any condensation, open the bag to air it out.

Per injera: 96 calories, 3 g protein, 1 g fat (0 g sat), 19 g carbohydrates, 39 mg sodium, 43 mg calcium, 3 g fiber

COOKING TIP: I prefer *injera* made from whole-grain brown teff flour, which produces a deep chocolate-brown color. If you want lighter-colored *injera* that look similar to those served in Ethiopian restaurants or that are sold in Ethiopian grocery stores (the ones sold in stores are generally cut with white flour or barley flour), be sure to purchase ivory teff flour (see page 9). This recipe can be halved, but since the batter is time-consuming to make, I recommend making a full batch.

TROUBLESHOOTING

- I've made *injera* dozens of times, and I've often noticed that mysteriously the first and last ones in a batch don't turn out that well. If that happens to you, don't be concerned; just toss them out or put them aside as a snack for the cook.

- The hardest part about making *injera* is finding the right cookware. I've found that *injera* stick terribly in cast iron, even in a well-seasoned pan. I've had great success using a flat, anodized metal griddle and also a ceramic-coated nonstick pan. I use a large lid from a stockpot to cover the pan so the *injera* can steam a bit as they cook.

- If you have a 14-inch nonstick pan, you can make larger *injera*. Use ⅓ cup of batter, and instead of spreading out the batter with a spoon, just tilt the pan around to spread it. Cover and cook as directed.

STORAGE TIP: *Injera* are best eaten the day they're made, but they'll stay fresh in a cool spot on the counter for a day or two. After that, store them in the fridge and use them for *Katenga* (page 66) or *fitfit* and *firfir* (see pages 147 to 152).

Mixed-Grain Injera

Injera are most commonly made from teff, but they're also frequently mixed with or made solely with other grains too. I've had success using 50 percent teff and 50 percent white rice flour or sorghum flour. The rice version has a chewier, stickier texture, so be careful when you stack the *injera*. Other than that, the method and directions are the same.

Although these crêpes don't have quite the same texture or pronounced sourness typical of teff *injera*, they make a good stand-in on days when you want Ethiopian food quickly and don't have time for the fermentation process or access to commercial *injera*. They have a slightly spongy-stretchy texture, with a small bit of tang from the yogurt and vinegar, and work well for scooping up sauces and stews.

quick teff crêpes

MAKES 14 (6-INCH) CRÊPES

1 cup **teff flour, any variety**

½ cup **chickpea flour**

½ teaspoon **baking soda**

½ teaspoon **salt**

2 cups **carbonated water**

⅔ cup **unsweetened plain vegan yogurt**

6 tablespoons **cider vinegar**

Preheat a nonstick skillet (see cooking tip) over medium heat.

Put the teff flour, chickpea flour, baking soda, and salt in a medium bowl and whisk vigorously to combine and to beat out any lumps in the chickpea flour. Add the carbonated water and vegan yogurt and whisk well to combine. When the griddle is hot, whisk in the vinegar to combine. The batter will rise and foam, and the consistency will be thin and reminiscent of chocolate milk.

Form each crêpe by using a ⅓-cup measure to scoop the batter from the bottom of the bowl and pour it into a disk on the hot pan. Use a spoon to quickly and lightly smooth the batter into a 6-inch disk, starting in the center and working in concentric circles until you reach the edges (keep the center of the crêpe the thickest and the edges the thinnest; the crêpe should be between ⅛ and ¼ inch thick).

Cover and cook for 1 minute. The crêpe should be dry on the top with a smattering of little holes over its surface. Uncover and continue to cook the crêpe without turning it for 1 to 1½ minutes. The total cooking time for each crêpe should be 2 to 2½ minutes. When fully cooked, the crêpe should be dry on top with a few air-bubble holes, and the bottom should be firm, smooth, and lightly browned. Depending on your cookware and stove, you'll need to adjust the heat to achieve this result. Use a flat, flexible spatula to loosen and release the crêpe, and then quickly transfer it to a plate and cover with a clean, dry tea towel. Repeat the cooking process until all the batter has been used. As the crêpes are made, stack them on top of

each other and keep them covered with the towel so they don't dry out.

As they cool, the crêpes will develop a spongy-stretchy texture. Let them rest until they're room temperature, then wrap the stack loosely in a clean, dry tea towel and seal it in a ziplock bag until serving time. Be sure the crêpes are completely cool or the bag will collect moisture and they'll spoil. If you notice any condensation, open the bag to air it out.

Per crêpe: 45 calories, 2 g protein, 1 g fat (0.3 g sat), 8 g carbohydrates, 97 mg sodium, 34 mg calcium, 2 g fiber

COOKING TIP: For the best success, I recommend cooking these crêpes on a flat, anodized griddle or pan. If you find the crêpes are sticking as they cook, mist the pan with a small amount of oil. Keep in mind, just as with traditional teff *injera*, the first one cooked is usually a throwaway or a treat for the cook.

COOKING TIP: Halve this recipe if you'd like a smaller yield, and for the best results, eat these the same day they're prepared.

2

This chapter is packed with recipes for the all-important basics: spice mixes, condiments, and other essentials that are vital to creating authentic Ethiopian flavors.

foundations

yib is a soft, uncultured cheese, similar in taste and texture to a mild ricotta. It's used as a condiment to balance and cool spicy dishes. It's also mixed into dishes to add creamy richness and tang. This vegan version is creamy, slightly lemony, and simple to make. *Ayib* is showcased

ayib

A SOFT, UNCULTURED VEGAN CHEESE

MAKES 2 CUPS

See photos facing pages 123 and 155

- 3 cups **unsweetened whole-fat soy milk**
  (see sidebar, page 37)

- ⅓ cup **raw cashew pieces, soaked in water for 3 hours and drained**
  (no need to soak if using a high-speed blender)

- ½ teaspoon **salt,** plus more if desired

- ¼ cup **freshly squeezed lemon juice**

  Freshly ground black pepper

Put the soy milk, cashews, and salt in a blender and process on high speed until creamy and smooth. Transfer to a medium saucepan and bring to a boil over medium-high heat, stirring occasionally (watch closely so it doesn't boil over). Immediately remove from the heat and add the lemon juice. Stir gently to just incorporate the lemon juice; the mixture will quickly curdle and thicken. Cover and let cool to room temperature undisturbed.

Strain through a fine-mesh sieve over the sink, discarding the liquid and retaining the curds in the sieve. Put the sieve over a bowl. Cover the sieve with a small plate and continue to drain the curds in the fridge until cold and thickened, at least 4 hours and up to 3 days (the cheese will get thicker and firmer the longer it drains).

Before serving, discard any additional liquid that has col lected in the bowl and transfer the cheese to a small dish. Season to taste with pepper and additional salt if desired (be generous with the salt, as it will balance the tang from the lemon juice). Serve immediately or cover and store in the fridge for up to 1 week.

Per ½ cup: 116 calories, 7 g protein, 7 g fat (1 g sat), 7 g carbohydrates, 193 mg sodium, 230 mg calcium, 2 g fiber

in several recipes, including Ye'kaysir Kitfo Be'ayib (page 140), in which it's mixed with roasted beets; the Italian-inspired Spicy Lasagna Roll-Ups (page 130); and *Ayib Be'gomen* (page 124), in which it's mixed with tender collard greens.

SERVING SUGGESTIONS

Serve a small, chilled scoop of *Ayib* alongside any of the spicier sauces or stews in the *Kay Wot* chapter (page 67); it's especially good with the hotter *Ye'telba Wot* (page 88) and *Ye'bedergan Wot* (page 82). *Ayib* is also great as a simple spread on crackers or toasted *injera* (see Katenga, page 66) and enjoyed as a snack.

Ayib be Mitmita (cheese with seasoned oil and hot spices): Season any amount of *Ayib* to taste with *Mitmita* (page 39) and a drizzle of *Ye'qimem Zeyet* (page 25).

Ayib be Timatim (cheese with tomatoes): Top ¼ cup of *Ayib* with 2 tablespoons of diced tomato that's been seasoned to taste with salt, freshly ground black pepper, and *Mitmita* (page 39) or cayenne.

Nut-Free Ayib: Omit the cashews and skip the blending step.

Which soy milk to use?

This recipe requires full-fat soy milk with no additives or fillers; the ingredients listed on the box should include only soybeans and water or soybeans, water, and salt. See the resources section (page 179).

Don't feel pressured to make homemade stock, as all the recipes in this book were tested using water with great results. However, if you want to amp up flavors, using a simple vegetable stock like this one can do the trick. You can make this any time of day, but my favorite method is to load up my slow cooker just before bedtime and then wake up to the smell of homemade stock wafting through my bedroom. At the risk of causing a riot, I'd say the aroma of homemade vegetable stock beats that of coffee.

sleepy vegetable stock

MAKES 10 CUPS

12 cups **water**

6 cups **coarsely chopped mixed vegetables**
(a combination of carrot, fennel, leek, onion, parsley, and tomato)

¼ cup **lentils, any variety**

Combine all the ingredients in a 5-quart slow cooker. Cover and cook on low for 8 to 10 hours. Alternatively, combine all the ingredients in a large stockpot and bring to a boil over high heat. Decrease the heat to medium, cover, and simmer until the stock is flavorful and the vegetables are very tender, 1 to 2 hours.

Strain and discard the solids. Use immediately or cool and store in a covered container in the fridge for up to 1 week.

STORAGE TIP: For longer storage, freeze the stock in 1-cup or 2-cup portions for easier use and faster thawing. Thaw before using.

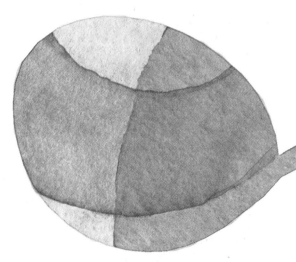

itmita is an intensely hot spice blend that's traditionally used to accompany Ethiopian meat dishes as a seasoning and condiment. Typically, it's made from ground bird's eye chiles, which are hotter than cayenne, but for my tastes, cayenne is plenty hot.

mitmita
A FIERY-HOT SPICE BLEND

MAKES ¼ CUP

4 tablespoons **cayenne**

½ teaspoon **ground cardamom**

½ teaspoon **ground cloves**

⅛ teaspoon **salt**

Combine all the ingredients in a small jar with a tight lid and shake to combine. Store in a cool, dark place for up to 4 weeks.

Per tablespoon: 19 calories, 1 g protein, 1 g fat (0.2 g sat), 3 g carbohydrates, 37 mg sodium, 10 mg calcium, 1 g fiber

SERVING SUGGESTIONS

If you're a fan of super-spicy food, put a small spoonful next to a few dishes on an *injera*-lined platter and dip into it as you eat. You can also season *Senafich* (page 44) with a pinch of *Mitmita* for a little extra oomph.

e'wot qimem (also known as *mekelesha* or *tikur qimem*) is a ground black-pepper spice blend used to season *kay wot* stews and sauces (see page 67). It has a sweet, inviting aroma, with a warm, peppery bite.

ye'wot qimem
A BLACK-PEPPER SPICE BLEND

MAKES 7 TABLESPOONS

1   teaspoon **organic canola oil or other neutral-tasting oil**

3   tablespoons **whole black peppercorns**

1   teaspoon **whole cloves**

1   tablespoon **whole nigella seeds** (see page 6)

½   teaspoon **husked green cardamom seeds**

½   teaspoon **whole cumin seeds**

2   teaspoons **ground cinnamon**

½   teaspoon **freshly grated nutmeg**

Heat the oil in a small skillet over medium-high heat. Add the peppercorns, cloves, nigella seeds, cardamom seeds, and cumin seeds. Toast the spices, stirring frequently, until fragrant and just starting to smoke, 2 to 3 minutes. Remove from the heat and quickly stir in the cinnamon and nutmeg. Transfer to a ceramic plate and let cool. Once cool, process into a fine powder using an electric coffee or spice grinder. Store in a tightly sealed container in a cool, dark place for up to 4 weeks.

Per tablespoon: 10 calories, 0 g protein, 1 g fat (0 g sat), 1 g carbohydrates, 0 mg sodium, 23 mg calcium, 1 g fiber

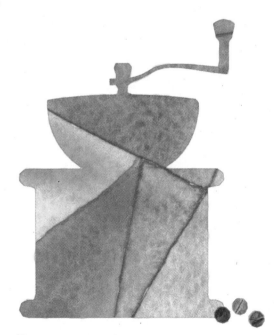

*A*waze is a *berbere*-based (see page 21) hot sauce that's traditionally used to season meat dishes and as a dipping condiment. While *awaze* variations are limitless, they frequently contain *berbere*, oil, water, garlic, and a little wine or liquor. *Awaze* may be used immediately, but it's even better after it sits in the fridge for a day or two so the flavors can blend.

awaze

RED PEPPER HOT SAUCE

MAKES ½ CUP

See photo facing page 58

- 3 tablespoons **ground *berbere*** (see page 21) **or *Berbere* Paste** (page 22; see cooking tip)
- 3 tablespoons **water**
- 4 teaspoons **freshly squeezed lime juice**
- 1 tablespoon **extra-virgin olive oil**
- 1 tablespoon **gin, whiskey, or table wine**
- 2 teaspoons **agave nectar**
- ½ teaspoon **granulated onion**
- ¼ teaspoon **peeled and grated fresh ginger**
- ¼ teaspoon **granulated garlic**

Put all the ingredients in a small bowl and stir until smooth and well combined. Serve immediately or store in a tightly covered container in the fridge for up to 1 week.

Per tablespoon: 27 calories, 0 g protein, 2 g fat (0 g sat), 2 g carbohydrates, 22 mg sodium, 0 mg calcium, 0 g fiber

Note: Because store-bought berbere spice will vary in ingredients, sodium levels may vary.

COOKING TIP: If you're using *Berbere* Paste, decrease the water to 2 tablespoons and add a pinch of salt.

SERVING SUGGESTIONS

Serve this as a dipping sauce with crunchy *Ye'misser Sambusas Be'ruz* (page 60) or *Ye'difin Misser Sambusas* (page 62). You can also use it as a marinade for *Awaze* Tofu (page 166) or serve it with any dish to impart a bit of Ethiopian-style heat and tang.

Dat'a is a raw, hot-pepper condiment that tastes like my mom's gazpacho ran off with the neighbor's Indian chutney and had a tasty baby. It's traditionally very spicy, but since I'm not a fan of burn-the-house-down heat, this version uses some mild Anaheim chiles to tone down the fire.

dat'a
SPICY GREEN-PEPPER RELISH

MAKES 1 CUP

See photos facing pages 58 and 123

- 3 **Anaheim chiles, seeded and coarsely chopped**
- 2 **jalapeño chiles, seeded, veined, and coarsely chopped**
- 2 tablespoons **freshly squeezed lime juice,** plus more if desired
- 4 cloves **garlic, pressed or grated** (2 teaspoons)
- 1 teaspoon **peeled and grated fresh ginger**
- ⅛ teaspoon **salt,** plus more if desired
- 1 cup **coarsely chopped fresh cilantro, lightly packed**

Put the Anaheim chiles, jalapeño chiles, lime juice, garlic, ginger, and salt in a food processor and process until smooth, stopping occasionally to scrape down the work bowl with a rubber spatula. Pulse in the cilantro, but don't overdo it; there should be visible bits of cilantro throughout the relish.

Taste and add more salt and a few more teaspoons of lime juice if desired. Store *Dat'a* in a tightly closed container in the fridge for up to 1 week.

Per 2 tablespoons: 12 calories, 1 g protein, 0 g fat (0 g sat), 2 g carbohydrates, 19 mg sodium, 3 mg calcium, 1 g fiber

COOKING TIP: Feel free to replace the chiles with whatever sort of hot green chiles you prefer. *Dat'a* can also be made from hot red chiles.

SERVING SUGGESTIONS

Serve *Dat'a* with any meal that could benefit from a little punch of vibrant, garlicky heat; a very small scoop is a pleasing accompaniment to a combo platter. I also like it spread on top of toasted *injera* (see *Katenga*, page 66), *Ye'shimbra Duket Kita* (page 50), *Ye'misser Sambusas Be'ruz* (page 60), *Ye'difin Misser Sambusas* (page 62), and *Awaze* Tofu (page 166).

ondiments are sort of my thing, so I decided to play around with the flavors of *dat'a* and came up with this version made from roasted vegetables and seasoned with *ajwain*. This variation is a good choice if you want a little kick of heat that's a bit smoother and milder than raw *Dat'a* (page 42). If you're not familiar with the taste of *ajwain*, this sauce will make a great introduction, as its taste shines through without overpowering the other flavors.

roasted dat'a

ROASTED GREEN-CHILE HOT SAUCE

MAKES 1 CUP

3 **Anaheim chiles, seeded and coarsely chopped**

2 **jalapeño chiles, seeded, veined, and coarsely chopped**

½ **yellow or white onion, coarsely chopped**

6 cloves **garlic**

½ teaspoon **whole *ajwain* seeds** (see page 4)

1 tablespoon **extra-virgin olive oil**

⅓ cup **water**

¼ cup **freshly squeezed lime juice**

6 **fresh basil leaves, or ¼ cup chopped fresh cilantro**

3 quarter-sized slices **ginger**

¼ teaspoon **salt,** plus more if desired

Preheat the oven to 475 degrees F. Line a baking sheet with parchment paper.

Put the Anaheim chiles, jalapeño chiles, onion, garlic, and *ajwain* seeds in a medium bowl. Add the oil and toss until evenly distributed. Arrange the vegetables in a single layer on the prepared baking sheet and bake for 15 minutes, until very tender and lightly charred.

Transfer to a blender. Add the water, lime juice, basil, ginger, and salt and process until smooth. Taste and add additional salt if desired. Let cool to room temperature.

Store *Roasted Dat'a* in a tightly closed container in the fridge for up to 1 week.

Per 2 tablespoons: 33 calories, 0 g protein, 2 g fat (0.2 g sat), 4 g carbohydrates, 1 mg sodium, 7 mg calcium, 1 g fiber

senafich

SPICY MUSTARD SAUCE

MAKES ⅓ CUP

¼ cup **whole-grain or stone-ground mustard**

1 tablespoon **water,** plus more if desired

2 teaspoons **extra-virgin olive oil**

1 clove **garlic**

Mitmita (page 39; optional)

Combine the mustard, water, oil, and garlic in a small food processor and process until smooth and somewhat creamy (there may still be bits of mustard seeds depending on the mustard you use). Season to taste with *Mitmita* if desired. If the mixture is too thick, add 1 to 2 teaspoons of additional water to achieve the desired consistency.

COOKING TIP: Instead of a food processor, put all the ingredients in a small glass measuring cup or drinking glass and process with an immersion blender. Alternatively, press the garlic, put all the ingredients in a small bowl, and whisk until smooth and emulsified.

Per 1 tablespoon: 38 calories, 0 g protein, 2 g fat (0.1 g sat), 2 g carbohydrates, 170 mg sodium, 0 mg calcium, 0 g fiber

SERVING SUGGESTIONS

Use this as a dipping sauce for *Ye'tofu Kwas* (page 160), Leftover Patties (page 168), *Ye'shimbra Duket Kita* (page 50), *Ye'misser Sambusas Be'ruz* (page 60), or *Ye'difin Misser Sambusas* (page 62), or serve it alongside any dish that could be enhanced by some garlicky mustard flavor.

Many Ethiopian restaurants in cities with large Ethiopian communities, such as Washington, DC, have a thriving breakfast scene. But since most traditional Ethiopian breakfast dishes aren't vegan, I stick to my BFF, the veggie combo, and make my own savory breakfast delights at home.

The breakfast dishes in this chapter should be served hot and are usually eaten with a crusty baguette and utensils. But if you'd prefer to eat them with injera, I won't give you the stink eye.

breakfast

Any variety of fava bean will yield tasty results in this recipe, but for the sake of authenticity, try to seek out small brown fava beans, also known as marrone or bell peas. You'll have the best luck finding them in well-stocked Middle Eastern grocery stores, since they're the same variety used to make *ful mudammas*, a similar fava bean dish prepared all over the Arab-speaking world.

shehan ful

TENDER, SEASONED FAVA BEANS TOPPED WITH TOMATOES, ONION, AND CHILE

MAKES 3½ CUPS

See photo facing page 26

- ½ **onion, diced** (1 cup)
- 2 tablespoons **extra-virgin olive oil,** plus more for drizzling
- 6 cloves **garlic, pressed or grated** (1 tablespoon)
- ½ teaspoon **salt,** plus more if desired
- 1 teaspoon **ground *berbere*** (see page 21) **or *Berbere* Paste** (page 22)
- ½ teaspoon **ground cumin**
- 3 cups **cooked or canned fava beans** (see cooking tip)
- 1 cup **water or Sleepy Vegetable Stock** (page 38)
- 1 small **tomato, diced** (⅓ to ½ cup)
- 2 tablespoons **minced green onion or other onion**
- 1 **jalapeño chile, seeded, veined, and minced**
- ¼ teaspoon **mild paprika**

   Cubed avocado, unsweetened plain vegan yogurt, or vegan sour cream, for garnish

Put the diced onion, oil, garlic, and salt in a medium saucepan and cook over medium-high heat, stirring frequently, until the onion has softened and is just beginning to brown, about 8 minutes. If the onion or garlic begins to stick, decrease the heat slightly. Stir in the *berbere* and cumin and cook for 1 minute. Add the the fava beans and water.

Increase the heat to high and bring to a boil. Decrease the heat to medium and simmer until the beans are very soft and the water has thickened into a light gravy, about 10 minutes. Mash using a large spoon or fork. The mixture should be mostly smooth but with some bean pieces throughout (similar to the texture of refried beans). Season to taste with additional salt if desired.

Spoon onto a platter or individual plates and sprinkle evenly with the tomato, green onion, chile, and paprika. Drizzle with olive oil and garnish with avocado.

Per ½ cup: 132 calories, 6 g protein, 4 g fat (1 g sat), 18 g carbohydrates, 88 mg sodium, 33 mg calcium, 5 g fiber

Note: Because store-bought berbere spice will vary in ingredients, sodium levels may vary.

COOKING TIP: Canned fava beans can be used in this recipe, but because they tend to be mealy, I recommend using home-cooked dried beans. Follow the instructions for cooking beans on page 13, but be aware that the small brown variety of fava beans has a tough skin and requires a longer cooking time to get soft (at least 2 hours on the stove top depending on the age and quality of the beans).

For cooking favas, I prefer to use a slow cooker, since the texture of the beans is better and they can cook overnight while I sleep. Put 1 cup of the small brown variety of fava beans in a slow cooker and add 7 to 8 cups of water. Cover and cook on high until very soft, 10 to 12 hours. Drain and discard the cooking water.

SERVING SUGGESTIONS

Shehan Ful is filling enough to be a stand-alone entrée, especially if it's served with a crusty baguette or *injera*, but if I'm making it for a special breakfast, I like to serve it with *Ye'tofu Enkulal Firfir* (page 48) and *Ye'shimbra Chechebsa* (page 51).

keep *Ye'qimem Zeyet* (page 25) in my fridge at all times, just so I'm able to make this dish at a moment's notice.

ye'tofu enkulal firfir
TOFU SCRAMBLE

MAKES 3 CUPS

See photo facing page 26

- ½ onion, **sliced ¼ inch thick and coarsely chopped** (¾ cup)
- 2 tablespoons **Ye'qimem Zeyet** (page 25) **or extra-virgin olive oil**
- 4 cloves **garlic, pressed or grated** (2 teaspoons)
- ½ teaspoon **salt,** plus more if desired
- 14 ounces **extra-firm tofu, rinsed and drained** (see cooking tip)
- 2 tablespoons **nutritional yeast flakes**
- 2 teaspoons **ground coriander**
- 1 teaspoon **ground *berbere*** (see page 21)
- ½ teaspoon **granulated onion**
- ¼ teaspoon **ground turmeric**
- 1 small **tomato, diced** (¾ cup)
- ¼ cup **minced fresh basil, lightly packed** (optional)
- ½ **jalapeño chile, cut into thin rounds**
- **Freshly ground black pepper**

Put the chopped onion, *Ye'qimem Zeyet*, garlic, and salt in a large skillet over medium-high heat and cook, stirring frequently, until the onion has softened, about 5 minutes.

Crumble the tofu (keeping some medium-sized chunks) into the skillet and sprinkle in the nutritional yeast, coriander, *berbere*, granulated onion, and turmeric. Stir to incorporate the spices into the tofu and cook, stirring frequently, until the tofu is lightly browned, 8 to 10 minutes. Add the tomato, optional basil, and chile and cook, stirring occasionally, until the tomato has softened slightly, about 2 minutes longer. Season to taste with pepper and additional salt if desired.

Per cup: 294 calories, 21 g protein, 21 g fat (3 g sat), 9 g carbohydrates, 212 mg sodium, 183 mg calcium, 3 g fiber

Note: Because store-bought berbere spice will vary in ingredients, sodium levels may vary.

COOKING TIP: Extra-firm tofu can vary in texture from brand to brand. If yours seems a bit soft and wet, gently squeeze out some of the liquid before using, or press it for 30 minutes (see page 7).

SERVING SUGGESTIONS

Serve *Ye'tofu Enkulal Firfir* as a main dish, as part of Special *Fata* (page 49), or alongside any of the other breakfast dishes in this chapter.

I n this dish, hearty bread is torn into pieces and tossed into a warm *kulet*, or spicy *berbere*-onion sauce, similar to a spicy bread stuffing. Warm, comforting, high-carb foods always make the best breakfasts, and *Dabo Firfir* is no exception; it's a popular and inexpensive way to start the day. To keep the bread from getting soggy, eat it immediately after you toss it into the hot sauce.

dabo firfir

BITS OF BREAD CRUMBLED INTO A SPICY SAUCE

MAKES 3 CUPS

½ small **red or yellow onion, minced** (¾ cup)

1 tablespoon **Ye'qimem Zeyet** (page 25) **or extra-virgin olive oil,** plus more for drizzling

½ teaspoon **salt,** plus more if desired

1 **jalapeño chile, seeded, veined, and sliced into thin half-moons**

4 cloves **garlic, pressed or grated** (2 teaspoons)

½ teaspoon **ground coriander**

2 tablespoons **ground *berbere*** (see page 21)

1½ cups **water or Sleepy Vegetable Stock** (page 38)

1 **baguette or crusty roll, coarsely chopped** (2½ cups), **or 4 thin *Ye'shimbra Duket Kita*** (page 50)

Put the onion, *Ye'qimem Zeyet*, and salt in a large skillet and cook over medium heat, stirring occasionally, until the onion is very soft, about 8 minutes. Add the chile, garlic, and coriander and stir to combine. Cook, stirring frequently, for 2 minutes. Stir in the *berbere*. Add the water, increase the heat to high, and bring to a boil. Decrease the heat to medium-high and simmer uncovered until the sauce has reduced to 1 cup, about 10 minutes.

Decrease the heat to low and keep the sauce warm until ready to serve. Add the baguette pieces and stir until thoroughly coated with the sauce and heated through. Drizzle with additional *Ye'qimem Zeyet* and season with additional salt if desired.

Per cup: 188 calories, 4 g protein, 5 g fat (1 g sat), 25 g carbohydrates, 198 mg sodium, 31 mg calcium, 1 g fiber

Note: Because store-bought berbere spice will vary in ingredients, sodium levels may vary.

Special *Fata:* Here's a great way to make an inexpensive and satisfying breakfast for a group of friends, especially if you also serve it with *Ye'beqolo Genfo* (page 52). Top a portion of *Dabo Firfir* with an equal portion of *Ye'tofu Enkulal Firfir* (page 48) and top with chopped avocado, unsweetened plain vegan yogurt, and minced green onions.

Injera Firfir: Replace the *Ye'shimbra Duket Kita* with finely torn *injera*.

Here's an Ethiopian version of an Indian flatbread I've enjoyed for many years. These savory pancakes make an excellent choice when you want a quick, low-fat, high-protein meal. There are endless ways to prepare these; for just a few, see the variations that follow. You can even use these pancakes as a quick scooping stand-in if you have no *injera*.

ye'shimbra duket kita

SAVORY CHICKPEA-FLOUR PANCAKES

MAKES 4 THIN PANCAKES, OR 2 THICK AND FLUFFY PANCAKES

1 cup **chickpea flour**

1 teaspoon **ground *berbere*** (see page 21) **or *Berbere* Paste** (page 22)

½ teaspoon **salt**

¼ teaspoon **ground coriander**

¼ teaspoon **ground cumin**

¼ teaspoon **ground turmeric**

¼ teaspoon **baking soda**

¾ cup **water**

1 teaspoon **peeled and grated fresh ginger**

1 teaspoon **freshly squeezed lemon juice**

Put the chickpea flour, ground *berbere* (if using *Berbere* Paste, add it with the water instead), salt, coriander, cumin, turmeric, and baking soda in a medium bowl and stir to combine. Add the water, ginger, and lemon juice and whisk until lump-free and smooth.

For thin pancakes, put about 1 teaspoon of organic canola oil in a large skillet over medium-high heat. When hot, add ¼ cup of the batter and use a spoon to gently spread the batter into a pancake that's 6 to 7 inches in diameter. Cook until the top is somewhat dry, bubbles appear in the center, and the bottom is brown, about 2 minutes. Decrease the heat if needed to prevent burning. Flip the pancake and cook until the other side is brown, about 2 minutes longer. Repeat with the remaining batter, adding more oil to the skillet for each pancake.

For thick and fluffy pancakes, put about 1 teaspoon of organic canola oil in a large skillet over medium-high heat. When hot, add ½ cup of the batter and let the pancake naturally spread into a round that's 5 to 6 inches in diameter. Cook until bubbles form around the edges of the pancake, the center has set up a bit, and the bottom is brown, about 5 minutes. Flip and cook until the other side is brown and the center is cooked through, about 3 minutes longer. Repeat with the remaining batter, adding another teaspoon of oil to the skillet for the second pancake.

Per 2 thin pancakes or 1 thick pancake: 188 calories, 11 g protein, 3 g fat (0.3 g sat), 29 g carbohydrates, 469 mg sodium, 32 mg calcium, 5 g fiber

Note: Because store-bought berbere spice will vary in ingredients, sodium levels may vary.

Ye'shimbra Chechebsa (savory pancakes with spicy seasoned oil): Cook the pancakes as directed. Mix 2 tablespoons of *Ye'qimem Zeyet* (page 25) with 2 teaspoons of ground *berbere* (see page 21) or *Berbere* Paste (page 22). Spread the *berbere* oil mixture evenly across the top of each pancake and cut into wedges before serving.

Ye'shimbra Kita Firfir (savory pieces of pancake tossed in spicy seasoned oil): Cook 4 thin pancakes. Tear them into small pieces and put them in a large bowl. Mix 2 tablespoons of *Ye'qimem Zeyet* (page 25) with 2 teaspoons of ground *berbere* (see page 21) or *Berbere* Paste (page 22). Drizzle over the torn pancakes until each piece is well coated with the *berbere* oil mixture. Eat with a spoon or fork as a snack (with a dollop of unsweetened plain vegan yogurt if you like), or serve for breakfast accompanied by *Shehan Ful* (page 46) and *Ye'tofu Enkulal Firfir* (page 48). Drizzle with agave nectar if a little sweetness is desired.

Ye'shimbra Kita Be'atakilt (savory vegetable-filled pancakes): Stir ½ cup of chopped tomato, ¼ cup of minced onion, and ¼ cup of minced fresh cilantro or basil into the batter and cook following the directions for the thick and fluffy pancakes (you may need to tilt the pan a little to help each pancake spread). These are great with a variety of different vegetables, such as shredded raw beet, sliced mushrooms, green onions, and green peas, so feel free to get creative.

COOKING TIP: Adjust the amount of oil to cook the pancakes depending on the type of skillet you use. For example, nonstick skillets will require less oil than other kinds of skillets.

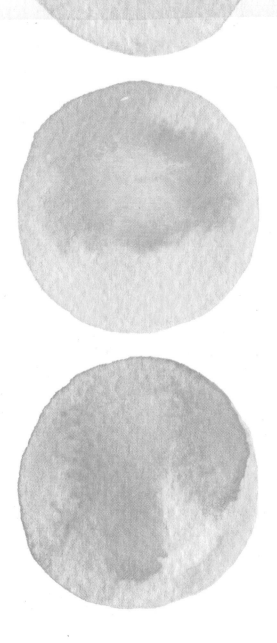

These grits turn me into a breakfast-chasing fool. I like them best served piping hot, when the cheese is melted and the *berbere* oil gets into every bite, but they're also excellent without the cheese. Leftovers reheat well in the microwave.

ye'beqolo genfo

CREAMY, CHEESY CORN GRITS WITH A SPICY SEASONED-OIL DRIZZLE

MAKES 2½ CUPS

See photo facing page 26

½ cup **organic yellow or white corn grits**

1 cup **water**

1 cup **unsweetened plain vegan milk**

½ teaspoon **salt,** plus more if desired

1 tablespoon ***Ye'qimem Zeyet*** (page 25)

½ to 1 teaspoon **ground *berbere*** (see page 21)

⅓ cup **grated vegan cheese** (optional)

Put the grits, water, vegan milk, and salt in a medium saucepan and stir to combine. Bring to a boil over high heat. While you're waiting for the grits to boil, put the *Ye'qimem Zeyet* and ½ teaspoon of the *berbere* in a small cup and stir to combine. Add more *berbere* to taste if desired.

Once the grits have come to a boil, decrease the heat to low and simmer gently, stirring frequently (be careful of hot splutters), until the grits have thickened considerably, about 5 minutes. Fold in the optional vegan cheese and continue to cook, stirring very gently or folding to keep the cheese intact, until the grits are smooth and creamy and have the consistency of loose mashed potatoes, about 5 minutes longer. Season to taste with additional salt if desired. Drizzle the *berbere* oil over the top before serving.

Per 1¼ cups: 271 calories, 6 g protein, 12 g fat (1 g sat), 33 g carbohydrates, 430 mg sodium, 153 mg calcium, 4 g fiber

Note: Because store-bought berbere spice will vary in ingredients, sodium levels may vary.

SERVING SUGGESTIONS

Besides making a filling meal any time of day, *Ye'beqolo Genfo* also works great as a side dish, especially when served with *Ye'abesha Gomen* (page 119) and *Awaze* Tofu (page 166), or any of the other savory breakfast dishes.

Genfo is a popular thick porridge eaten for breakfast. It's commonly made from wheat or barley flour, but I use sorghum flour to keep it gluten-free. This recipe is very filling and makes enough for a generous portion, but you can easily double it to make more. Serve *Genfo* hot with a spoon, dipping small portions into the *berbere* oil before eating.

ye'mashila genfo

THICK SORGHUM PORRIDGE WITH A SPICY SEASONED OIL

MAKES 1½ CUPS

See photo facing page 26

¾ cup **sorghum flour**

1½ cups **water**

¾ teaspoon **salt**

1 tablespoon **Ye'qimem Zeyet** (page 25), **warmed**

½ teaspoon **ground *berbere*** (see page 21), plus more if desired

Unsweetened plain vegan yogurt, for garnish

Put the sorghum flour in a medium saucepan and toast it over medium-high heat, stirring frequently, for 2 minutes. Add the water and salt and beat out any lumps with a big spoon or whisk. Decrease the heat to medium and cook, stirring constantly (it will get quite thick), until the sorghum is perfectly smooth, has the consistency of very stiff mashed potatoes, and no longer tastes raw, 8 to 10 minutes.

Mound the porridge into a small bowl and use your hands or a spoon to form the top into a rounded dome with a shallow well in the center. Mix the warm *Ye'qimem Zeyet* with the *berbere*, adding up to ½ teaspoon additional *berbere* to taste if desired. Pour the *berbere* oil into the well. Serve garnished with vegan yogurt if desired.

Per ¾ cup: 273 calories, 6 g protein, 10 g fat (1 g sat), 38 g carbohydrates, 475 mg sodium, 2 mg calcium, 5 g fiber

Note: Because store-bought berbere spice will vary in ingredients, sodium levels may vary.

created these pancakes as a way to use up extra *Ersho* (page 28), but now I make *Ersho* just so I can make these pancakes. (The batter makes great waffles, too.) They're tangy and golden brown, mottled with bubbles from the fermented starter. If you omit the fruit and store the batter covered in the fridge, the pancakes will be even fluffier the next day; simply add the berries right before you cook them.

blueberry-cinnamon sourdough pancakes

MAKES 9 (5-INCH) PANCAKES

1 cup **unsweetened plain vegan milk**

2 tablespoons **organic canola oil,** plus more for cooking

2 tablespoons **finely ground flaxseeds**

2 teaspoons **pure vanilla extract**

1 cup **sorghum flour**

2 tablespoons **tapioca starch or cornstarch**

2 tablespoons **unbleached granulated sugar**

2 teaspoons **baking powder**

1 teaspoon **ground cinnamon**

½ teaspoon **salt**

½ cup ***Ersho*** (page 28)

¾ cup **fresh or frozen blueberries**

Maple syrup, for drizzling

Put the vegan milk, oil, flaxseeds, and vanilla extract in a small bowl and stir to combine. Let sit for 5 minutes.

Put the sorghum flour, tapioca starch, sugar, baking powder, cinnamon, and salt in a medium bowl and stir to combine.

Stir the vegan milk mixture. Then add the vegan milk mixture and *Ersho* to the flour mixture. Stir well with a large spoon to combine. Preheat a flat, anodized metal griddle or nonstick skillet over medium-low heat for 5 to 10 minutes while the batter rests. Just before cooking the pancakes, gently stir the blueberries into the batter.

Lightly coat the griddle with oil. For each pancake, scoop out ⅓ cup of batter and pour it on the griddle. Cook each pancake until the bottom is deep golden brown, the edges are set, and the top has a few bubbles in the center and is mostly dry, 3 to 4 minutes. Flip with a spatula and cook the other side until the pancake is cooked through and golden brown on both sides, about 2 minutes longer. Repeat with the remaining batter. Serve hot with a drizzle of maple syrup.

Per pancake: 102 calories, 2 g protein, 4 g fat (0.3 g sat), 14 g carbohydrates, 143 mg sodium, 56 mg calcium, 2 g fiber

Blueberry-Cinnamon Sourdough Waffles: Thicken the batter slightly with an additional 2 tablespoons of flour.

Wheat-Flour Sourdough Pancakes: Replace the sorghum flour and tapioca starch with 1 cup of unbleached all-purpose flour.

4

This chapter is packed with recipes for hot and cold appetizers and crunchy snacks that make great party food or accompaniments to coffee, tea, and chatter.

appetizers
and snacks

This recipe makes a Middle Eastern–style hummus with a few Ethiopian-inspired twists. Please don't confuse this with *elibet*, a dish made with fermented broad beans and sunflower seeds that's often referred to as Ethiopian hummus; they're completely different.

Ethiopian-style hummus

MAKES 1½ CUPS

½ cup plus 1 teaspoon **shelled raw sunflower seeds**

1½ cups **cooked or canned chickpeas** (see cooking tip)

¼ teaspoon **salt,** plus more if desired

⅓ cup **water**

2 cloves **garlic**

1 teaspoon **grated lemon zest**

3 tablespoons **freshly squeezed lemon juice**

1 teaspoon **ground *berbere*** (see page 21)

1 teaspoon **seeded, veined, and minced jalapeño chile** (optional)

2 teaspoons **extra-virgin olive oil**

Put the sunflower seeds in a large skillet and toast them over medium-high heat, stirring almost constantly (don't walk away, as they can burn in the blink of an eye), until the seeds are light golden brown, about 4 minutes. Immediately remove from the heat. Set aside 1 teaspoon of the seeds for a garnish and transfer the remaining ½ cup of seeds to a food processor. Process, stopping frequently to scrape the sides and bottom of the work bowl with a rubber spatula, until the seeds are pulverized and turn into seed butter. Depending on your machine, this can take 4 to 7 minutes, but it will happen quickly once the seeds fully release their oil.

Add the chickpeas and salt and process until the chickpeas are pulverized and form a ball with the seed butter. Add the water, garlic, lemon zest, and lemon juice and process until smooth and creamy. Season with additional salt to taste if desired and transfer to a small serving bowl or plate.

Smooth the top of the hummus with the back of a small spoon, and then use the spoon to form a shallow well. Do this by making concentric circles in the center as you press down lightly, guiding the displaced hummus to the sides where it will form a slight wall. Sprinkle the *berbere* and optional chile into the well, then drizzle the oil over the hummus and garnish with the reserved teaspoon of sunflower seeds. Alternatively, mix the oil and *berbere* in a small bowl and drizzle the mixture over the chile.

Cover and refrigerate until cold. Tightly covered, Ethiopian-Style Hummus can be stored in the fridge for up to 1 week.

Per ¼ cup: 113 calories, 5 g protein, 5 g fat (1 g sat), 13 g carbohydrates, 64 mg sodium, 30 mg calcium, 4 g fiber
Note: Because store-bought berbere spice will vary in ingredients, sodium levels may vary.

COOKING TIP: One 15-ounce can of chickpeas will yield just enough for this recipe. Rinse and drain the chickpeas before using.

SERVING SUGGESTIONS

Ethiopian-Style Hummus can be eaten however you enjoy traditional hummus—with flatbread, in a sandwich, with apple slices (my favorite), or with vegetables for dipping. It's also great spread onto toasted *injera* (see *Katenga*, page 66), rolled up and cut into pinwheels so you can easily pop them into your mouth.

ere's a riff on traditional *dabo kolo*, a crunchy snack composed of small pieces of slightly sweet wheat dough, fried until crunchy. This recipe makes a more seasoned and somewhat addictive baked snack, with a crunchy sesame seed coating and a hint of spice from the *berbere* and cin-

dabo kolo

CRUNCHY, SALTY, SPICY, AND SWEET BREADSTICK BITES

MAKES 4 CUPS

1¼ cups **chickpea flour**

1 cup **oat flour**

¾ cup **teff flour**

3 tablespoons **ground *berbere*** (see page 21)

2 teaspoons **salt**

2 teaspoons **granulated onion**

½ teaspoon **ground cinnamon**

½ cup **sweet potato purée** (see sidebar, page 59)

¼ cup **extra-virgin olive oil**

¼ cup **water,** plus more if needed

1 tablespoon **agave nectar**

⅓ cup **raw sesame seeds**

Preheat the oven to 350 degrees F. Line a baking sheet with parchment paper.

Put the chickpea flour, oat flour, teff flour, *berbere*, salt, granulated onion, and cinnamon in a large bowl and stir to combine. Add the sweet potato purée, oil, water, and agave nectar and stir with a large spoon to form a thick, soft, and somewhat sticky dough. Use your hands to knead the dough directly in the bowl, incorporating in any remaining flour to form a smooth, cohesive ball. If the dough seems dry, add additional water, a few teaspoons at a time, until the dough comes together.

Divide the dough into quarters and cover with a clean, dry tea towel to keep it from drying out. Spoon one-quarter of the sesame seeds into a small pile on a flat surface. Take one-quarter of the dough, form it into a thick log, and roll it in the sesame seeds. Keep rolling the dough in the seeds until the entire log is covered and the seeds are embedded in the dough. Form the dough into a long, thin rope, about ½ inch thick (to make it easier to handle, you can cut the rope in half as you work). Use a dull knife to cut the rope into small pieces, ½ to ¾ inches long. Wipe the knife on a clean towel when it gets sticky.

Arrange the pieces in a single layer on the prepared baking sheet and repeat with the remaining dough and seeds. Bake for 30 to 35 minutes, turning the pieces with a spatula every 10 minutes, until deep brown and somewhat crunchy (they'll become crunchier as they cool).

Clockwise from top: **Ye'difin Misser Sambusas,** *page 62;* **Dat'a,** *page 42;* **Ye'kaysir Kitfo Be'ayib,** *page 140;*
Fancy Katenga Pinwheels, *page 66 variation;* **Awaze,** *page 41*

Clockwise from top: **Timatim Fitfit,** *page 134 variation;* **Selata,** *page 132;* **Butecha,** *page 139;*
Senig Karia Be'timatim, *page 143;* **Bozena Shiro,** *page 110*

namon. While these are a little labor intensive to make, they can be a fun afternoon or evening project and are totally worth the effort. If you've never worked with a gluten-free dough before, take your time while you roll these out; the dough is easy to work with but doesn't have the same stretch as a dough made with wheat flour.

Cool completely, then transfer to an airtight container. Store *Dabo Kolo* tightly covered at room temperature for up to 1 week.

Per ½ cup: 295 calories, 9 g protein, 13 g fat (2 g sat), 35 g carbohydrates, 556 mg sodium, 111 mg calcium, 7 g fiber
Note: Because store-bought berbere spice will vary in ingredients, sodium levels may vary.

SERVING SUGGESTIONS

Enjoy *Dabo Kolo* with a cup of hot coffee or *Shai Be'qimem* (page 171). For party fare, *Dobo Kolo* mixes well with roasted peanuts.

Sweet Potato Purée

To make sweet potato purée, put a cooked, skinned sweet potato in a food processor and process until smooth. If you're baking sweet potatoes (see page 13), bake an extra one for this recipe, or simply peel, cube, and steam a sweet potato until soft and tender.

Sambusas are similar to Indian samosas, except instead of the expected potato filling, they're usually stuffed with meat or lightly seasoned lentils that are wrapped in a thin wheat pastry. These sambusas are filled with tender lentils and mushrooms in a spiced red gravy, and instead of the

ye'misser sambusas be'ruz

CRISPY RICE-PAPER PASTRIES WITH
A SPICED LENTIL-TOMATO FILLING

MAKES 18 SAMBUSAS

5 cups **water**

1 cup **dried red lentils**

½ **red onion, minced** (1 cup)

½ teaspoon **salt,** plus more if desired

2 cups **thickly sliced mushrooms**

3 tablespoons *Ye'qimem Zeyet* (page 25) **or extra-virgin olive oil**

2 cloves **garlic, pressed or grated** (1 teaspoon)

2 tablespoons **ground *berbere*** (see page 21) **or *Berbere* Paste** (page 22)

1 tablespoon **mild paprika**

1 teaspoon **ground cumin**

¼ teaspoon **ground cinnamon**

1 **tomato, diced** (1 cup)

3 tablespoons **unsalted tomato paste**

Freshly ground black pepper

9 (8-inch) **rice papers** (see page 10)

1 tablespoon **organic canola oil**

To make the lentil filling, put the water and lentils in a medium-large saucepan and bring to a boil over high heat. Stir to prevent the lentils from sticking to the bottom of the pan. Decrease the heat to medium-low and simmer uncovered, skimming off any foam that forms on the top with a large spoon. Cook, stirring every few minutes, until the lentils are soft but not mushy, about 10 minutes. Drain the lentils and reserve 2 tablespoons of the cooking water.

While the lentils cook, put the onion and salt in a large saucepan. Cover and cook over medium-high heat, stirring often, for 5 minutes. Add the mushrooms, *Ye'qimem Zeyet,* and garlic and stir well to combine. Cook uncovered, stirring often, until the mushrooms have softened and released their liquid, about 3 minutes.

Add the *berbere,* paprika, cumin, and cinnamon and stir well to incorporate the spices into the oil, about 30 seconds, then add the tomato and tomato paste. Cook, stirring often, until the tomato has softened, about 5 minutes.

Stir in the lentils and reserved cooking water and stir well to combine. Simmer until the mixture is reduced to a thick stew, 15 to 20 minutes. Season to taste with pepper and additional salt if desired. Set aside to cool and thicken.

To fill and bake the *sambusas*, preheat the oven to 375 degrees F. Line a baking sheet with parchment paper.

Lay a clean, dry tea towel on the counter or table where you intend to work (preferably near the sink), smoothing it flat. Working with one sheet of rice paper at a time, put the rice paper under warm running water, directing the water first on top of the paper, then the underside, and then the top again, for a total of about 5 seconds. Let the rice paper drip in the sink for a

traditional fried crust, they're baked in rice-paper wrappers, which are an inexpensive and easy gluten-free twist. This rice-paper version is quite different from *Ye'difin Misser Sambusas* (page 62). They'll also be easier to whip out in bulk for that vegan Ethiopian-themed potluck you have looming around the corner.

second, then put the moistened rice paper on top of the towel and quickly arrange it so it's completely flat.

Cut the rice paper into equal halves using a sharp knife or pizza cutter. Put 2 heaping tablespoons of the lentil filling in the center of one of the rice-paper halves. Grab a corner and bring it over the filling, and repeat with the other side. Be sure to overlap the two sides, which will form a cone-like shape with a pointed bottom. Fold the bottom edge up and over the filling to enclose the packet and form a triangle-shaped *sambusa*. Carefully transfer the *sambusa* to the prepared baking sheet and repeat with the remaining rice papers and filling. As you transfer each one to the baking sheet, be careful they don't touch (they'll stick together and create holes when you try to pull them apart).

Brush each *sambusa* with a very thin coating of oil (the *sambusas* will crisp best with the thinnest amount of oil), then carefully flip and coat the other side. Bake for 10 minutes, until the bottoms are light brown and the shells begin to firm. Flip gently and continue baking, turning them every few minutes for 13 to 20 minutes, until golden brown and crispy on all sides. Serve hot.

Per sambusa: 80 calories, 3 g protein, 3 g fat (0.3 g sat), 11 g carbohydrates, 127 mg sodium, 10 mg calcium, 2 g fiber

Note: Because store-bought berbere spice will vary in ingredients, sodium levels may vary.

SERVING SUGGESTIONS

Lentil-filled *sambusas* are commonly served with a little schmear of *Awaze* (page 41), but you can dip them into any condiment you like, including *Senafich* (page 44), *Dat'a* (page 42), or Roasted *Dat'a* (page 43).

Vegetable Sambusas: Instead of the lentil filling, use any of the cooked vegetable recipes in this book. However, decrease the amount of liquid in the recipe so the filling won't be too juicy.

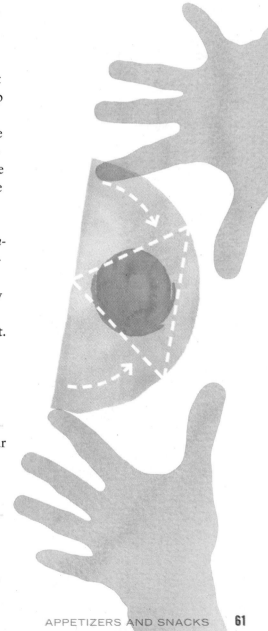

raditionally, meat-free *sambusas* are filled with lentils, but I love filling these with all kinds of things, especially leftovers (see variations below).

ye'difin misser sambusas

CRUNCHY, LENTIL-STUFFED PASTRIES WITH A CHICKPEA-FLOUR CRUST

MAKES 8 SAMBUSAS

See photo facing page 58

- 2¼ cups **chickpea flour,** plus more for dusting if needed
- 1½ teaspoons *Berbere* **Paste** (page 22), **or** 1 teaspoon **ground** *berbere* (see page 21)
- ½ teaspoon **salt**
- ¼ teaspoon **ground turmeric**
- ⅓ cup **water**
- ¼ cup **extra-virgin olive oil,** plus more for oiling
- 2 cups **Lentil** *Sambusa* **Filling** (page 65)

Preheat the oven to 375 degrees F. Line a baking sheet with parchment paper and oil the parchment paper.

Put the chickpea flour, *berbere*, salt, and turmeric in a large bowl and stir to combine. Pour in the water and oil and stir to form a thick dough. Using your hands, knead the dough directly in the bowl, incorporating any stray flour and forming a smooth cohesive ball.

Divide the dough into quarters. Roll each quarter into a ball and cover the balls with a clean, dry tea towel so they don't dry out while you work. Roll each ball into a ⅛-inch-thick disk, dusting it with chickpea flour if necessary to prevent sticking. Alternatively, roll out each disk on a piece of parchment paper. Cut the disk in half and form a cone from each semicircle, overlapping the edges slightly to form a seam. Pinch the seam gently to seal and fill the cone with ¼ cup of filling. Pinch the top of the cone closed and fold it over, pinching gently to seal. Put the *sambusa* on the prepared baking sheet and repeat with the remaining dough.

Brush each *sambusa* on both sides with oil. Bake for 12 minutes, until the bottoms are brown. Flip the *sambusas* over and bake for 10 to 12 minutes longer, until golden brown and crispy on both sides.

Per sambusa: 247 calories, 11 g protein, 11 g fat (1 g sat), 28 g carbohydrates, 112 mg sodium, 60 mg calcium, 10 g fiber

Note: Because store-bought berbere spice will vary in ingredients, sodium levels may vary.

TROUBLESHOOTING

The chickpea-flour dough should be somewhat moist and easy to roll out without being crumbly or sticky. If the dough seems a bit dry or crumbly, add up to 2 tablespoons of water, 1 to 2 teaspoons at a time, until it's easier to roll out. Take care not to add too much water, since the dough should be easy to roll out without sticking. If the dough seems too wet, knead in an additional tablespoon of chickpea flour.

SERVING SUGGESTIONS

Serve these *sambusas* hot with a dipping sauce, such as *Awaze* (page 41) and Roasted *Dat'a* (page 43).

VARIATIONS: Instead of Lentil *Sambusa* Filling, try these stuffed with Ethiopian-Style Mac 'n' Cheesie (page 126), *Ye'ater Kik Alicha* (page 96), *Ye'abesha Gomen* (page 119), or *Ayib Be'gomen* (page 124).

olo is a crunchy snack often made from cooked beans or boiled and roasted grains, such as barley, wheat, or oats. This variation is crunchy, spicy, and a little zippy.

ye'shimbra be'akuri ater kolo
CRUNCHY, SPICY CHICKPEAS AND SOYBEANS

MAKES 2 CUPS

- 2 cups **cooked or canned chickpeas** (see cooking tip)
- 1¼ cup **canned white or black soybeans** (see cooking tip)
- 2 tablespoons *Ye'qimem Zeyet* (page 25) **or extra-virgin olive oil**
- 1 tablespoon **freshly squeezed lime juice**
- 4 teaspoons **ground** *berbere* (see page 21)
- 1 teaspoon **ground coriander**
- ½ teaspoon **salt,** plus more if desired

Preheat the oven to 400 degrees F. Line a baking sheet with parchment paper.

Put all the ingredients in a medium bowl and toss until the beans are evenly coated. Transfer the beans to the prepared baking sheet and arrange them in a single layer. Bake for 45 to 55 minutes, stirring every 10 to 12 minutes, until the beans are very dry, deep golden brown, and verging on crunchy (don't let the spices burn).

When cool enough to handle, taste and season with more salt if desired. Let cool to room temperature (they'll get crunchier as they cool). Serve immediately, or store in a tightly closed container at room temperature for up to 1 week.

Per ½ cup: 353 calories, 7 g protein, 9 g fat (1 g sat), 23 g carbohydrates, 560 mg sodium, 42 mg calcium, 7 g fiber
Note: Because store-bought berbere spice will vary in ingredients, sodium levels may vary.

COOKING TIP: For ease of preparation and to save time, I prefer to use canned beans rather than home-cooked beans for this recipe. One 25-ounce can of chickpeas yields 2 cups. One 15-ounce can of soybeans yields about 1¼ cups. Rinse and drain canned beans before using. If you have difficulty locating canned soybeans, use shelled edamame, which can be found in the freezer aisle of well-stocked supermarkets.

SERVING SUGGESTIONS

Ye'shimbra Be'akuri Ater Kolo makes a satisfying snack with tea, especially if roasted peanuts are added to the mix. It's also great sprinkled over salad.

ere's a mild-mannered lentil filling for stuffing into *Ye'difin Misser Sambusas* (page 62). You'll probably be tempted to snack on this, but force yourself not to because it makes just enough for eight sambusas.

lentil sambusa filling

MAKES 2 CUPS

2 cups **water or Sleepy Vegetable Stock** (page 38)

½ cup **dried brown or green lentils**

⅓ cup **diced onion**

1 tablespoon **extra-virgin olive oil**

2 cloves **garlic, slivered** (1 tablespoon)

2 cups **baby spinach, lightly packed**

Pinch **freshly grated nutmeg**

Salt

Freshly ground black pepper

Put the water and lentils in a medium saucepan and bring to a boil over high heat. Stir to prevent the lentils from sticking to the bottom of the pan. Decrease the heat to medium-low, cover, and simmer, stirring occasionally, until the lentils are tender but not mushy, about 15 minutes. Drain and discard the cooking liquid.

Put the onion and oil in a separate medium saucepan and cook over medium-high heat, stirring frequently, for 3 minutes. Decrease the heat to medium-low, add the garlic, and cook, stirring frequently, for 5 minutes.

Add the spinach and stir to combine. Cover and cook just long enough to wilt the spinach, 1 to 2 minutes. Remove from the heat and stir in the lentils and nutmeg. Season to taste with salt and pepper.

Per ¼ cup: 62 calories, 4 g protein, 2 g fat (0.2 g sat), 8 g carbohydrates, 9 mg sodium, 15 mg calcium, 4 g fiber

Toasting is the perfect way to handle extra or day-old *injera*, as it transforms the texture into a chewy delight.

katenga

TOASTED INJERA BRUSHED WITH SPICY SEASONED OIL

MAKES 8 PIECES

See photo facing page 58

- 1 tablespoon **Ye'qimem Zeyet** (page 25) **or extra-virgin olive oil, warmed**
- ½ to 1 teaspoon **ground berbere** (page 21) **or Berbere Paste** (page 22)
- 1 (16-inch) **commercial injera,** or 3 (7-inch) **homemade injera** (page 30)

Preheat the oven to 300 degrees F. Line a baking sheet with parchment paper.

Put the *Ye'qimem Zeyet* and *berbere* in a small bowl and stir to combine.

Put the *injera* bubble-side up on the prepared baking sheet. Make sure it's not bunched or rolled in any area (or touching another piece of *injera* if you're baking more than one at a time). Bake until the edges are a little crisp and the *injera* is slightly firmer, about 10 minutes.

Brush the top of the *injera* with the spiced oil. Roll the *injera* into a tight log and slice it into bite-sized pinwheels.

Per piece: 31 calories, 1 g protein, 2 g fat (0.2 g sat), 3 g carbohydrates, 37 mg sodium, 7 mg calcium, 0 g fiber

Note: Because store-bought berbere spice will vary in ingredients, sodium levels may vary.

Fancy Katenga Pinwheels: Spread a piece of toasted *injera* with the spiced oil and then add a thin layer of *Ayib* (page 36), *Ayib Be'gomen* (page 124), Ethiopian-Style Hummus (page 56), Special *Ye' Kaysir Kitfo Be'ayib* (page 140), or any leftover *wot* (see page 70) that's in your fridge. Roll the *injera* tightly into a log, and then slice it into bite-sized pinwheels.

In this chapter, I've organized all the important information and recipes you'll need to become an expert at making spicy red *wot* (see page 16). If you haven't already done so, head over to the *berbere* info page (see page 21) and read all about this epic spice blend; it's essential for this type of dish, whether you buy it or make it yourself.

5

kay wot
SPICY RED SAUCES AND STEWS

When cooking *kay wot*, a red spicy sauce is made first, followed by the addition of the main ingredients, which are simmered in the sauce until they're done. This sauce is called *kulet*, and there's a bit of a formula to making it. Once you read through the recipes and make a few of them, you'll recognize the pattern. In the meantime, here's a breakdown to help you understand the backbone of these recipes.

BASIC *KAY WOT* STEPS

1. Finely minced red onion or shallots are mixed with salt and cooked in a hot, dry pan until they sweat and soften. This step will help them break down into the sauce or gravy, which is important to the finished texture of the sauce.

2. *Ye'qimem Zeyet* (page 25) is added to the onion, and then the onion is cooked further until very soft.

3. Seasonings are added: spices, garlic, ginger, and sometimes tomatoes or tomato paste.

4. Water, stock, or alcohol is added and the mixture is brought to a boil. Then the heat is decreased and the mixture is simmered until the onion has broken down into the liquid, creating the *kulet*, or sauce.

5. The main ingredient is added and the stew is cooked until everything is tender, the flavors are blended, and the sauce has reduced and thickened.

6. The *kay wot* is seasoned to taste and then served hot or warm with *injera*.

A NOTE ABOUT *KAY WOT* INGREDIENTS

Ye'wot Qimem

As you peruse the *kay wot* recipes, you'll notice they all contain an optional spice blend called *Ye'wot Qimem* (page 40). This blend of peppery and warm spices is quick and easy to make if you have an electric spice grinder; you can also find it ready-made in Ethiopian specialty stores. While it does add a little something-something to the stews and sauces, it's not super noticeable, and the recipes have been written to be fabulous with or without it.

Onion

Traditionally, red onions or shallots are used in *kay wot*, but feel free to use whatever you have on hand. To help the onions break down into the *kulet*, they should be very finely minced. Using a food processor is an easy way to do this while also saving precious time and tears. Just be sure to decrease the amount of onion each recipe calls for by a smidge, as the amounts specified in the recipes are based on hand-minced onion: 1 medium onion, minced by hand = 2 cups; 1 medium onion, machine processed = 1½ cups.

Berbere and You

Kay wot is definitely meant to have some kick, and these recipes are what I'd describe as moderately hot. Since all *berbere* is different, I suggest making a recipe as written and then adjusting the amount of *berbere* as desired for the next recipe. If you want something milder, decrease the *berbere* in a recipe by 1 tablespoon and replace it with mild paprika. If you want something spicier, replace any paprika in the recipe with *berbere* and add even more if you like your food extra hot. If you cook with both imported *berbere* and *Berbere* Paste (page 22), you'll notice the stews made with the homemade paste will be lighter in color but not less spicy or less flavorful.

Like other ground spices, *berbere* burns pretty easily, so once it's added to the cooked onion, be sure to have the liquid measured and ready to go so you can add it quickly. You'll notice that some of the recipes call for a small amount of beer or wine. If you avoid alcohol, simply replace the booze with an equal amount of water or broth. And if you're boozalicous, feel free to experiment with any of the alcohol-free recipes by replacing ½ cup of the water or broth with whatever you've got bubbling in the garage.

Salt

In order to adjust for salt variances in different *berbere* blends (homemade versus commercial products) and different oil bases (plain oil versus commercial vegan butters) in *Ye'qimem Zeyet*, these recipes have all been developed with the least amount of salt. Please adjust the salt of each finished *wot* to taste.

POINTS TO KEEP IN MIND

Wot are often considered sauces rather than stews, and it's important to remember this, particularly if you're making a dish that's new or unfamiliar. These dishes should have lots of gravy, and when spooned onto a blanket of *injera*, they should spread, rather than hold their shape and stay in firm mounds. Don't be afraid to add extra liquid as necessary to thin the consistency of your dish (especially with all of the legume dishes). If you add too much liquid, there are a few tricks you can use to thicken it up again:

1. Increase the heat so the *wot* cooks at a rapid simmer, but don't step away from the stove because the *wot* could quickly scorch.

2. Take the saucepan off the heat and cover it. Let the *wot* rest for 5 to 10 minutes; you'll be surprised how quickly it thickens.

3. Refrigerate the *wot* and reheat it after it's been thoroughly chilled.

SERVING AND SCOOPING

Kay wot is meant to be served hot, warm, or room temperature, with fresh *injera* and a variety of other dishes. If you're struggling with a recipe that's too spicy for your taste, know that the *berbere* will mellow the longer it simmers and rests, so it will be noticeably milder after resting for several hours. The contrasting tang from *injera* will also cool it down, as will milder, creamy foods like *Ayib* (page 36), *Butecha* (page 139), *Ye'souf Fitfit* (page 149), *Ye'selit Fitfit* (page 150), a mild *alicha wot* (see page 93), or even just the simple addition of chopped avocado sprinkled with salt.

LEFTOVERS

Kay Wot stores like a champ if it's covered tightly and kept in the fridge. Like other stewed foods, it's even better the next day, once the flavors have had a chance to mingle. It will most likely thicken in the fridge, so simply stir in a little extra water before heating it up. I usually do this in a small saucepan on the stove or in a ceramic bowl in the microwave. If you have lots of extras, try turning some of your leftovers into Leftover Patties (page 168) or use them as a filling for crunchy, stuffed *sambusas* (pages 60 and 62).

his spicy, flavorful stew has both a lot of eye appeal and texture.

ye'atakilt wot

POTATOES, CARROTS, AND CAULIFLOWER IN A SPICY SAUCE

MAKES 5 CUPS

See photo facing page 154

- 1 **small red onion, minced** (1½ cups)
- ½ teaspoon **salt,** plus more if desired
- 3 tablespoons *Ye'qimem Zeyet* (page 25) **or extra-virgin olive oil**
- 1 **small tomato, diced** (¾ cup)
- 4 cloves **garlic, pressed or grated** (2 teaspoons)
- 1 teaspoon **ground coriander**
- ½ teaspoon *Ye'wot Qimem* (page 40; optional)
- ¼ teaspoon **ground turmeric**
- ⅛ teaspoon **ground cardamom**

  Pinch **ground cloves**
- 3 tablespoons **ground** *berbere* (see page 21) **or** *Berbere* **Paste** (page 22)
- 1 tablespoon **mild paprika**
- 1½ pounds **cauliflower, cut into bite-sized florets** (4 cups)
- 1 **large carrot, peeled and cut into sticks** (1 cup; see page 13)
- 1 **thin skinned potato, peeled and cut into bite-sized chunks** (1 cup)
- 1½ cups **water or Sleepy Vegetable Stock** (page 38)

Put the onion and salt in a large, dry saucepan. Cover and cook over medium-high heat, stirring occasionally to prevent sticking and burning, until the onion has released its liquid and softened, about 5 minutes. Decrease the heat to medium, add the *Ye'qimem Zeyet*, and stir to combine. Cover and cook, stirring occasionally, until the onion is very soft and beginning to brown, about 10 minutes. If the onion sticks or begins to burn, decrease the heat slightly. Stir in the tomato, garlic, coriander, optional *Ye'wot Qimem*, turmeric, cardamom, and cloves. Cover and cook, stirring frequently, until the tomato is soft but still chunky, about 5 minutes.

Stir in the *berbere* and paprika. Add the cauliflower, carrot, and potato and stir to coat with the spices. Add the water. Increase the heat to high and bring to a boil. Decrease the heat to medium, cover, and simmer, stirring frequently, until the vegetables are tender and the sauce has thickened, about 20 minutes.

Per cup: 219 calories, 6 g protein, 10 g fat (1 g sat), 27 g carbohydrates, 831 mg sodium, 85 mg calcium, 7 g fiber

Note: Because store-bought berbere spice will vary in ingredients, sodium levels may vary.

COOKING TIP: I like the cauliflower in this recipe cooked until very tender, but if you prefer yours firmer, cook the potatoes together for about 5 minutes, before adding the cauliflower.

Ye'atakilt Firfir (spicy vegetable stew with *injera*): Put a portion of the *wot* in a medium saucepan and heat over medium-low heat until hot. Add about twice as much chopped or torn *injera* as *wot* and cook, stirring frequently, until the *injera* has absorbed the sauce and softened and is heated through.

This spicy, hearty, and comforting stew can be found on veggie platters in virtually every Ethiopian restaurant.

ye'misser wot

RED LENTILS IN A SPICY SAUCE

MAKES 4 CUPS

See photos facing pages 122 and 123

- 1 cup **dried red lentils**
- 5 cups **water**
- 1 **red onion, minced** (2 cups)
- ½ teaspoon **salt,** plus more if desired
- 3 tablespoons **Ye'qimem Zeyet** (page 25) **or extra-virgin olive oil**
- 6 cloves **garlic, pressed or grated** (1 tablespoon)
- 1 teaspoon **peeled and grated fresh ginger**
- ½ teaspoon **Ye'wot Qimem** (page 40; optional)
- ¼ teaspoon **ground cumin**
- ⅛ teaspoon **ground cardamom**
- 3 tablespoons **ground *berbere*** (page 21) **or *Berbere* Paste** (page 22)
- 1 tablespoon **mild paprika**
- 2 cups **reserved cooking water or Sleepy Vegetable Stock** (page 38), plus more if needed

Put the lentils and water in a large saucepan and bring to a boil over high heat. Stir to keep the lentils from sticking to the bottom of the pan. Decrease the heat to medium and simmer uncovered, skimming off any foam that forms on the top with a large spoon. Cook, stirring occasionally, until the lentils are tender but firm, 8 to 10 minutes. Drain and reserve the cooking water.

Put the onion and salt in a large, dry saucepan. Cover and cook over medium-high heat, stirring occasionally to prevent sticking and burning, until the onion has released its liquid and softened, about 5 minutes. Decrease the heat to medium, add the *Ye'qimem Zeyet*, and stir to combine, scraping up any onion that has stuck to the bottom of the pan. Cover and cook, stirring occasionally, until the onion is very soft and beginning to brown, about 10 minutes longer. If the onion is sticking or burning, decrease the heat slightly. Add the garlic, ginger, optional *Ye'wot Qimem*, cumin, and cardamom and cook, stirring frequently, for 1 minute.

Stir in the *berbere* and paprika. Add 2 cups of the reserved lentil cooking water. Bring to a boil over high heat. Decrease the heat to medium, cover, and simmer, stirring frequently, until the sauce has thickened slightly and the onion has begun to break down into the sauce, about 5 minutes. Stir in the lentils and up to ½ cup additional cooking water if needed to thin the sauce.

Cover, decrease the heat to medium-low, and simmer gently, stirring frequently, until the lentils and onion have broken down into the sauce and the sauce pools a little on top, 5 to 10 minutes. The finished *wot* should have a thick sauce, similar to a chowder. Season to taste with additional salt if desired.

Per cup: 334 calories, 15 g protein, 12 g fat (2 g sat), 44 g carbohydrates, 155 mg sodium, 108 mg calcium, 11 g fiber

Note: Because store-bought berbere spice will vary in ingredients, sodium levels may vary.

Ye'ater Kik Wot (split peas in a spicy sauce): Replace the red lentils with dried yellow split peas. Increase the water to 7 cups and cook until tender but firm, 20 to 30 minutes. Drain, reserving the cooking water, and proceed with the recipe as directed.

See photo facing page 91

his easy variation of *Ye'misser Wot* (page 72) contains more *berbere* since the addition of tomato tempers the heat a bit. Don't be afraid to thin this out with extra water; it should be saucy and thick like a chowder and spread when you spoon it on top of *injera*.

ye'misser wot be'timatim

RED LENTILS IN A SPICY TOMATO SAUCE

MAKES 5 CUPS

- 1 cup **dried red lentils**
- 5 cups **water**
- 1 **red onion, minced** (2 cups)
- ½ teaspoon **salt,** plus more if desired
- 3 tablespoons **Ye'qimem Zeyet** (page 25) **or extra-virgin olive oil**
- 6 cloves **garlic, pressed or grated** (1 tablespoon)
- 1 teaspoon **peeled and grated fresh ginger**
- 1 teaspoon **ground coriander**
- ½ teaspoon **Ye'wot Qimem** (page 40; optional)
- ⅛ teaspoon **ground cardamom**
- 4 tablespoons **ground *berbere*** (page 21) **or *Berbere* Paste** (page 22)
- 1 tablespoon **mild paprika**
- 2 tablespoons **unsalted tomato paste**
- 1 **tomato, diced** (1 cup)
- 2 cups **reserved lentil cooking water or Sleepy Vegetable Stock** (page 38), plus more if needed

Put the lentils and water in a large saucepan and bring to a boil over high heat. Stir to keep the lentils from sticking to the bottom of the pan. Decrease the heat to medium and simmer uncovered, skimming off any foam that forms on the top with a large spoon. Cook, stirring occasionally, until the lentils are tender but firm, 8 to 10 minutes. Drain and reserve the cooking water.

Put the onion and salt in a large, dry saucepan. Cover and cook over medium-high heat, stirring occasionally to prevent sticking and burning, until the onion has released its liquid and softened, about 5 minutes. Decrease the heat to medium, add the *Ye'qimem Zeyet*, and stir to combine, scraping up any onion that has stuck to the bottom of the pan. Cover and cook, stirring occasionally, until the onion is very soft and is beginning to brown, about 10 minutes. If the onion sticks or begins to burn, decrease the heat slightly. Add the garlic, ginger, coriander, optional *Ye'wot Qimem*, and cardamom and cook, stirring frequently, for 1 minute.

Stir in the *berbere* and paprika. Add the tomato paste and stir constantly for 1 minute. Stir in the tomato and 2 cups of the reserved lentil cooking water. Increase the heat to high and bring to a boil. Decrease the heat to medium, cover, and simmer, stirring frequently, until the sauce has thickened slightly and the onion and tomatoes have begun to break down, about 5 minutes. Stir in the lentils and up to ½ cup of additional lentil cooking water if needed to thin the sauce.

Cover and simmer gently, stirring frequently, until the onion has broken down into the sauce and the sauce pools a little on top, 5 to 10 minutes longer. Season to taste with additional salt if desired.

Per cup: 191 calories, 13 g protein, 0 g fat (0 g sat), 36 g carbohydrates, 122 mg sodium, 63 mg calcium, 9 g fiber
Note: Because store-bought berbere spice will vary in ingredients, sodium levels may vary.

Ye'ater Kik Wot Be'timatim (split peas in a spicy tomato sauce): Replace the red lentils with dried yellow split peas. Increase the water to 7 cups and cook until tender but firm, 20 to 30 minutes. Drain, reserving the cooking water, and proceed with the recipe as directed.

his tasty twist on *Ye'misser Wot* (page 72) includes tender bites of sliced okra. The tomato and okra mellow the fiery bite from the *berbere*, so if you like your *kay wot* on the mild side, this one's a good choice.

ye'misser wot be'bamya
RED LENTILS WITH OKRA IN A SPICY TOMATO SAUCE

MAKES 5 CUPS

1 cup **dried red lentils**

5 cups **water**

½ **red onion, minced** (1 cup)

½ teaspoon **salt,** plus more if desired

3 tablespoons *Ye'qimem Zeyet* (page 25) **or extra-virgin olive oil**

1½ cups **sliced fresh or frozen okra,** in ½-inch segments

1 **large tomato, diced** (1½ cups)

4 cloves **garlic, pressed or grated** (2 teaspoons)

1 teaspoon **peeled and grated fresh ginger**

½ teaspoon *Ye'wot Qimem* (page 40; optional)

⅛ teaspoon **ground cardamon**

Pinch **ground cloves**

3 tablespoons **ground *berbere*** (see page 21) **or *Berbere* Paste** (page 22)

1 tablespoon **mild paprika**

2 cups **reserved cooking water or Sleepy Vegetable Stock** (page 38), plus more if desired

Freshly ground black pepper

Put the lentils and water in a large saucepan and bring to a boil over high heat. Stir to keep the lentils from sticking to the bottom of the pan. Decrease the heat to medium and simmer uncovered, skimming off any foam that forms on the top with a large spoon. Cook, stirring occasionally, until the lentils are tender but firm, 8 to 10 minutes. Drain and reserve the lentil cooking water.

Put the onion and salt in a large, dry saucepan. Cover and cook over medium-high heat, stirring occasionally to prevent sticking and burning, until the onion has released its liquid and softened, about 5 minutes. Decrease the heat to medium, add the *Ye'qimem Zeyet*, and stir to combine, scraping up any onion that has stuck to the bottom of the pan. Cover and cook, stirring occasionally, until the onion is very soft and beginning to brown, about 10 minutes. If the onion is sticking or burning, decrease the heat slightly.

Add the okra, tomato, garlic, ginger, optional *Ye'wot Qimem*, cardamom, and cloves and stir to combine. Cover and cook, stirring frequently, until the tomatoes have broken down and the okra has softened, 10 to 12 minutes. Stir in the *berbere* and paprika. Stir in 2 cups of the reserved lentil cooking water. Increase the heat to high and bring to a boil. Decrease the heat to medium-low, cover, and simmer, stirring frequently, until the okra is very tender, about 10 minutes. Stir in the lentils and up to ½ cup additional lentil cooking water if needed to thin the sauce.

Cover and simmer gently, stirring frequently, until the sauce pools a little on top, 5 to 10 minutes longer. Season to taste with pepper and additional salt if desired.

Per cup: 274 calories, 13 g protein, 9 g fat (0 g sat), 33 g carbohydrates, 648 mg sodium, 63 mg calcium, 10 g fiber

Note: Because store-bought berbere spice will vary in ingredients, sodium levels may vary.

COOKING TIP: Okra can be hard to find in cooler climates, so I purchase frozen sliced okra in bags from the grocery store. There's no need to defrost the okra. Simply toss it in with the fresh tomatoes.

ith the addition of sautéed mushrooms, this red lentil *wot* is a little fancier than most.

ye'misser wot be'ingudai
RED LENTILS WITH MUSHROOMS IN A SPICY SAUCE

MAKES 5 CUPS

1 cup **dried red lentils**

5 cups **water**

½ **red onion, minced** (1 cup)

½ teaspoon **salt,** plus more if desired

3 tablespoons ***Ye'qimem Zeyet*** (page 25) **or extra-virgin olive oil**

6 cloves **garlic, pressed or minced** (1 tablespoon)

2 teaspoons **ground coriander**

1 teaspoon **peeled and grated fresh ginger**

½ teaspoon ***Ye'wot Qimem*** (page 40; optional)

Pinch **ground cardamom**

Pinch **ground cloves**

3 tablespoons **ground *berbere*** (see page 21) **or *Berbere* Paste** (page 22)

1 tablespoon **mild paprika**

2 cups **reserved cooking water or Sleepy Vegetable Stock** (page 38), plus more if desired

8 ounces **button mushrooms, thickly sliced** (4 cups)

Put the lentils and water in a large saucepan and bring to a boil over high heat. Stir to keep the lentils from sticking to the bottom of the pan. Decrease the heat to medium and simmer uncovered, skimming off any foam that forms on the top with a large spoon. Cook, stirring occasionally, until the lentils are tender but firm, 8 to 10 minutes. Drain and reserve the lentil cooking water.

Put the onion and salt in a large, dry saucepan. Cover and cook over medium-high heat, stirring occasionally to prevent sticking and burning, until the onion has released its liquid and softened, about 5 minutes. Decrease the heat to medium, add 2 tablespoons of the *Ye'qimem Zeyet*, and stir to combine, scraping up any onion that has stuck to the bottom of the pan. Cover and cook, stirring occasionally, until the onion is very soft and beginning to brown, about 10 minutes. If the onion sticks or begins to burn, decrease the heat slightly. Add the garlic, coriander, ginger, optional *Ye'wot Qimem*, cardamom, and cloves and cook, stirring frequently, for 1 minute.

Stir in the *berbere* and paprika. Add 2 cups of the reserved lentil cooking water. Increase the heat to high and bring to a boil. Cover and decrease the heat to medium. Simmer, stirring frequently, until the sauce has thickened slightly and the onion has begun to break down into the sauce, about 5 minutes. Stir in the lentils and up to ½ cup additional lentil cooking water if needed to thin the sauce. Simmer uncovered, stirring frequently, until the sauce has thickened and pools a little on top, about 15 minutes.

While the stew simmers, heat a large saucepan over medium-high heat. Add the remaining tablespoon of *Ye'qimem Zeyet* and the mushrooms. Cook, stirring frequently, until the mushrooms have softened and are lightly brown, 5 to 7 minutes. Just before serving, season the lentils to taste with additional salt if desired and top with the mushrooms.

Per cup: 274 calories, 13 g protein, 9 g fat (1 g sat), 32 g carbohydrates, 645 mg sodium, 34 mg calcium, 9 g fiber

Note: Because store-bought berbere spice will vary in ingredients, sodium levels may vary.

Milk made from toasted sunflower seeds adds creaminess and a roasted flavor that's unusual in other Ethiopian *wot*. This dish reminds me of a West African groundnut stew, and while spicy, it's also extremely rich, which tempers much of the heat.

ye'ater kik wot be'souf

SPLIT PEAS IN A SPICY SAUCE WITH MILK MADE FROM TOASTED SUNFLOWER SEEDS

MAKES 6 CUPS

1 cup **dried yellow split peas**

9½ cups **water**

1¾ cups **shelled raw sunflower seeds**

1 **large red onion, minced** (2½ cups)

¾ teaspoon **salt,** plus more if desired

4 tablespoons *Ye'qimem Zeyet* (page 25) **or extra-virgin olive oil**

½ teaspoon *Ye'wot Qimem* (page 40; optional)

1 **tomato, diced** (1 cup)

6 cloves **garlic, pressed or grated** (1 tablespoon)

2 teaspoons **peeled and grated fresh ginger**

4 tablespoons **ground *berbere*** (see page 21) or *Berbere* **Paste** (page 22)

½ cup **reserved cooking water or Sleepy Vegetable Stock** (page 38), plus more if desired

Put the split peas and 7 cups of the water in a large saucepan and bring to a boil over high heat. Stir to prevent the peas from sticking to the bottom of the pan. Decrease the heat to medium and simmer uncovered, skimming off any foam that forms on the top with a large spoon. Cook, stirring occasionally, until the peas are soft but firm, about 30 minutes. Drain and reserve the cooking water.

Put the sunflower seeds in a large skillet and toast over medium-high heat, stirring frequently, until light golden brown and fragrant, 10 to 12 minutes. Immediately remove from the heat and transfer to a food processor. Process until the seeds are pulverized and begin to release their oil, about 2 minutes, stopping occasionally to scrape down the sides and bottom of the work bowl with a rubber spatula. The seeds are sufficiently processed when they clump together slightly when pressed between your fingers. Don't overprocess the seeds or you'll end up with sunflower seed butter.

Add the remaining 2½ cups of water to the food processor and process for 20 seconds. Set a fine-mesh sieve over a bowl and pour the contents of the food processor into the sieve. Let the sunflower seed milk drain into the bowl. Using a metal spoon, scrape and press the seeds and pulp against the inside of the strainer. Use some pressure to extract as much milk as possible from the seeds, and scrape the thick sunflower cream that accumulates on the underside of the sieve into the bowl. This process should take 2 to 5 minutes of continuous scraping; the resulting milk will be a little thicker than other nondairy milks and very slightly gritty. Pour the milk into a measuring cup and if necessary add enough reserved cooking water to make 2½ cups.

Put the onions and salt in a large, dry saucepan. Cover and cook on medium-high heat, stirring occasionally to prevent sticking and burning, until the onions have released their liquid and softened, about 5 minutes. Decrease the heat to medium, add the *Ye'qimem Zeyet*, and stir to combine, scraping up any onion that has stuck to the bottom of the pan. Cover and cook, stirring occasionally, until the onions are very soft and beginning to brown, about 10 minutes. If the onions stick or begin to burn, decrease the heat slightly. Add the optional *Ye'wot Qimem* and stir constantly for 30 seconds. Add the tomato, garlic, and ginger. Cover and cook, stirring frequently, until the tomato has broken down and formed a thick sauce, about 5 minutes.

Stir in the *berbere*. Then stir in the sunflower milk and split peas. Simmer uncovered over medium-low heat, stirring frequently (be careful of hot splutters), for 10 minutes. Stir in ½ cup of the reserved cooking water to thin the sauce. If the sauce gets too thick, add up to ½ cup of additional cooking water if needed to thin it. Continue to simmer and stir until the split peas are tender and small pools of oil have risen to the surface, about 10 minutes longer. The *wot* should have the consistency of a thick chowder.

Per cup: 441 calories, 17 g protein, 31 g fat (3 g sat), 34 g carbohydrates, 532 mg sodium, 73 mg calcium, 13 g fiber
Note: Because store-bought berbere spice will vary in ingredients, sodium levels may vary.

Ye'misser Wot Be'souf (red lentils in a spicy sauce with milk made from toasted sunflower seeds): Replace the split peas with dried red lentils. Cook in 5 cups of water until tender, 8 to 10 minutes. Drain, reserving the cooking water, and proceed with the recipe as directed. *(See photo facing page 155.)*

his stew is among the spicier dishes in this book and a bit more time-consuming to make, but it's totally worth the extra investment, especially if you're going all out for a special occasion. The slow-cooked onions and spices create an especially flavorful sauce that is

ye'bedergan wot

BUTTERY-SOFT ROASTED EGGPLANT IN A SPICY SAUCE

MAKES 5 CUPS

See photo facing page 91

- 1½ pounds **eggplant, stem removed and skin pierced several times with a fork**
- 2 **red onions, minced** (4 cups)
- ½ teaspoon **salt,** plus more if desired
- ¼ cup ***Ye'qimem Zeyet*** (page 25) **or extra-virgin olive oil**
- 6 cloves **garlic, pressed or grated** (1 tablespoon)
- 1 teaspoon **peeled and grated fresh ginger**
- ½ teaspoon **ground cumin**
- ½ teaspoon ***Ye'wot Qimem*** (page 40; optional)
- 1 **tomato, peeled and diced** (1 cup)
- 4 tablespoons **ground *berbere*** (see page 21) **or *Berbere* Paste** (page 22)
- 2 tablespoons **mild paprika**
- 3 cups **water or Sleepy Vegetable Stock** (page 38)

Preheat the oven to 425 degrees F. Line a baking sheet with parchment paper.

Put the whole eggplant on the prepared baking sheet and bake for 30 to 40 minutes, turning it with tongs several times to promote even baking, until it has collapsed and is very soft. Remove from the oven and let rest until cool enough to handle. Cut the eggplant in half laterally and discard the skin (it should slip off easily). Chop the eggplant into 1-inch pieces.

While the eggplant bakes, put the onions and salt in a large, dry saucepan. Cover and cook over medium-low heat, stirring frequently to prevent sticking and burning, until the onions are soft and translucent, about 30 minutes. The onions will sweat and release their liquid.

Increase the heat to medium and stir in the *Ye'qimem Zeyet*. Cover and cook, stirring frequently, until the onions are very soft, about 15 minutes longer. Stir in the garlic, ginger, cumin, and optional *Ye'wot Qimem*. If the onions stick or begin to burn, decrease the heat slightly. Cover and cook, stirring frequently, for 3 minutes longer.

punctuated with chunks of buttery-soft eggplant. The longer this simmers, the better the flavors come together. If you have time, cover it and keep it simmering gently over very low heat while you prepare other dishes.

Stir in the tomato, *berbere*, and paprika. Cover and cook, stirring frequently, until the tomato has broken down and formed a thick sauce, about 5 minutes. Stir in the water. Increase the heat to high and bring to a boil. Decrease the heat to medium, cover, and simmer, stirring frequently, until the sauce has thickened, about 15 minutes. Add the eggplant and simmer for 15 minutes.

Per cup: 215 calories, 3 g protein, 12 g fat (2 g sat), 31 g carbohydrates, 826 mg sodium, 75 mg calcium, 6 g fiber

Note: Because store-bought berbere spice will vary in ingredients, sodium levels may vary.

Ye'bedergan Firfir (spicy eggplant stew with *injera*): Put a portion of *wot* in a medium saucepan and heat over medium-low heat until hot. Add about twice as much chopped or torn *injera* as *wot* and cook, stirring frequently, until the *injera* has absorbed the sauce and softened and is heated through.

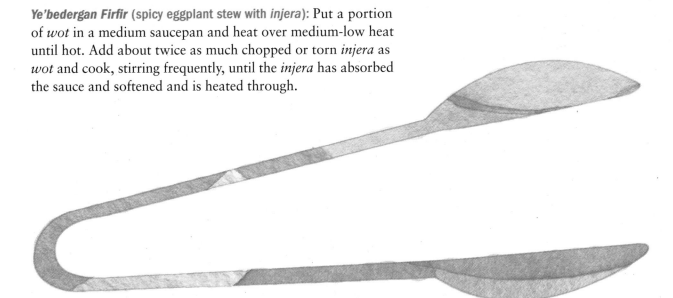

This saucy *wot* has all the flavors you could want in a spicy fall stew, plus you get to finish off a bottle of beer while you make it. For a completely gluten-free version, use gluten-free beer.

ye'dubba wot

ROASTED BUTTERNUT SQUASH IN A SPICY SAUCE

MAKES 3 CUPS

1¼ pounds **butternut squash, peeled and cut into 1-inch pieces** (3 rounded cups)

2½ tablespoons **Ye'qimem Zeyet** (page 25) **or extra-virgin olive oil**

½ **red onion, minced** (1 cup)

½ teaspoon **salt,** plus more if desired

4 cloves **garlic, pressed or grated** (2 teaspoons)

2 teaspoons **peeled and grated fresh ginger**

¼ teaspoon **ground cinnamon**

¼ teaspoon **Ye'wot Qimem** (page 40; optional)

⅛ teaspoon **ground allspice**

⅛ teaspoon **ground cardamom**

⅛ teaspoon **ground cloves**

3 tablespoons **ground berbere** (page 21) **or Berbere Paste** (page 22)

1 tablespoon **mild paprika**

1 cup **lager beer**

1 cup **water or Sleepy Vegetable Stock** (page 38)

Freshly ground black pepper

Preheat the oven to 425 degrees F. Line a baking sheet with parchment paper.

Put the squash in a large bowl and sprinkle it with a pinch of salt. Drizzle 1½ teaspoons of the *Ye'qimem Zeyet* over the squash and use your hands to toss the squash until it is well coated. Arrange the squash in a single layer on the prepared baking sheet. Bake for 20 to 30 minutes, until tender and lightly brown.

Put the onion and salt in a large, dry saucepan. Cover and cook over medium-high heat, stirring occasionally to prevent sticking and burning, until the onion has released its liquid and softened, about 5 minutes. Decrease the heat to medium, add the remaining 2 tablespoons of *Ye'qimem Zeyet*, and stir to combine, scraping up any onion that has stuck to the bottom of the pan. Cover and cook, stirring occasionally, until the onion is very soft and beginning to brown, about 10 minutes. If the onion sticks or begins to brown, decrease the heat slightly. Add the garlic, ginger, cinnamon, optional *Ye'wot Qimem*, allspice, cardamom, and cloves and cook, stirring frequently, for 1 minute.

Stir in the *berbere* and paprika. Add the beer and water. Increase the heat to high and bring to a boil. Decrease the heat to medium, cover, and simmer, stirring frequently, until the sauce has thickened slightly and the onion has begun to break down into the sauce, 5 to 10 minutes. Stir in the squash and partially cover the saucepan. Simmer, stirring frequently, until the sauce has thickened to the consistency of a thin marinara, about 15 minutes longer. Season to taste with pepper and additional salt if desired.

Per cup: 288 calories, 3 g protein, 13 g fat (2 g sat), 31 g carbohydrates, 1,229 mg sodium, 116 mg calcium, 6 g fiber

Note: Because store-bought berbere spice will vary in ingredients, sodium levels may vary.

SERVING SUGGESTIONS

Serve this *wot* with other comforting dishes, such as mild, creamy *Ye'ater Kik Alicha* (page 96) and buttery-soft stewed *Ye'tikil Gomen Be'karot* (page 123) or *Ye'tikil Gomen Be'timatim* (page 122).

This traditional fasting *wot* is a bit more time-intensive to make than most of the others, but it's one of my favorites. If you're lucky, you might even find it on the menu at your neighborhood Ethiopian joint. *Ye'shimbra asa* translates to "chickpea fish," and traditionally a chickpea-flour dough is molded or rolled and cut into fish shapes, baked or fried until crisp, and added to the spicy sauce in which they soften.

ye'shimbra asa wot

CHICKPEA-FLOUR CRACKERS IN A SPICY WINE SAUCE

MAKES 6 CUPS

chickpea-flour crackers

1 tablespoon **organic canola oil**

2¼ cups **chickpea flour**

1½ teaspoons **ground *berbere*** (see page 21) **or *Berbere* Paste** (page 22)

½ teaspoon **salt**

¼ teaspoon **ground turmeric**

⅓ cup **water**

¼ cup **extra-virgin olive oil**

sauce

1½ **red onions, minced** (3 cups)

¾ teaspoon **salt,** plus more if desired

¼ cup ***Ye'qimem Zeyet*** (page 25) **or extra-virgin olive oil**

6 cloves **garlic, pressed or grated** (1 tablespoon)

½ teaspoon **ground cumin**

½ teaspoon ***Ye'wot Qimem*** (page 40; optional)

⅛ teaspoon **ground cardamom**

3 tablespoons **ground *berbere*** (see page 21) **or *Berbere* Paste** (page 22)

1 tablespoon **mild paprika**

2½ cups **water or Sleepy Vegetable Stock** (page 38)

½ cup **table wine**

Freshly ground black pepper

To make the crackers, preheat the oven to 375 degrees F. Line a baking sheet with parchment paper and oil the parchment paper with the canola oil.

Put the chickpea flour, *berbere*, salt, and turmeric in a large bowl and stir well to combine. Pour in the water and olive oil and stir to form a thick dough. Using your hands, knead the dough directly in the bowl, incorporating any stray flour and forming a smooth, cohesive ball.

Put a piece of parchment paper on the counter or a flat surface and put the dough on it. Pat the dough into a thick disk, then roll it out so it's ¼ inch thick. Cut the dough into hearts, fish, or whatever shapes suit your fancy using small cookie cutters.

Transfer the cutouts to the prepared baking sheet and bake for 10 minutes. Carefully turn the pieces over and bake for 8 to 10 minutes longer, until baked through, golden brown, and crispy. Let cool while you prepare the sauce.

To make the sauce, put the onions and salt in a large, dry saucepan. Cover and cook over medium heat, stirring occasionally to prevent sticking and burning, until the onions have released their liquid and softened, about 10 minutes.

Decrease the heat to medium-low, add the *Ye'qimem Zeyet*, and stir to combine, scraping up any onion that has stuck to the bottom of the pan. Cover and cook, stirring occasionally, until the onions are very soft, about 15 minutes. Add the garlic, cumin, optional *Ye'wot Qimem*, and cardamom and cook, stirring frequently, for 1 minute.

Stir in the *berbere* and paprika. Add the water and wine. Increase the heat to high and bring to a boil. Decrease the heat to medium, cover, and simmer, stirring frequently, until the onions have broken down and the sauce has reduced and thickened into a gravy, about 30 minutes.

Carefully submerge the crackers in the sauce. Decrease the heat to medium-low, cover, and simmer gently until the crackers have softened and are hot, 10 to 15 minutes. Season to taste with pepper and additional salt if desired.

Per cup: 403 calories, 10 g protein, 25 g fat (3 g sat), 30 g carbohydrates, 977 mg sodium, 68 mg calcium, 9 g fiber

Note: Because store-bought berbere spice will vary in ingredients, sodium levels may vary.

COOKING TIP: If you're planning to make this dish ahead of time, be aware that the crackers will continue to soften and eventually fall apart the longer they sit in the sauce (that's one of my favorite things about this dish). If you want the crackers to be firmer and more intact, keep them separate from the sauce until serving time. Shortly before serving, heat the sauce over medium heat, adding a little water if necessary to thin it. When the sauce is simmering, carefully add the crackers and simmer just until the crackers have softened and are heated through, 10 to 15 minutes.

TROUBLESHOOTING

The chickpea-flour dough should be somewhat moist and easy to roll out without being crumbly or sticky. If the dough seems a bit dry or crumbly, add up to 2 tablespoons of water, 1 to 2 teaspoons at a time, until it's easier to roll out. Take care not to add too much water, since the dough should be easy to roll out without sticking. If the dough seems too wet, knead in an additional tablespoon of chickpea flour.

Dumpling Wot: Replace the chickpea-flour crackers with 20 *Ye'tofu Kwas* (page 160) or *Ye'shimbra Duket Kwas* (page 162).

Ye'shimbra Asa Firfir (injera in a spicy wine sauce): Put a portion of *wot* in a medium saucepan and heat over medium-low heat until hot. Add about twice as much chopped or torn *injera* as *wot* and cook, stirring frequently, until the *injera* has absorbed the sauce and softened and is heated through.

When toasted, flaxseeds become surprisingly nutty and delicious, with a rich aroma and flavor. In this *wot*, the toasted ground flaxseeds blend into the *kulet* and transform it into a rich, luscious sauce reminiscent of peanut butter, Mexican *mole*, and chocolate. The raw jalapeño chile adds a crunchy contrast to the smooth sauce, but if it's too spicy for your taste, just leave it out. This *wot* will mellow if you make it a few hours ahead and reheat it before serving.

ye'telba wot

A RICH, SPICY SAUCE MADE FROM TOASTED, GROUND FLAXSEEDS

MAKES 2 CUPS

See photo facing page 90

- ⅓ cup **whole brown flaxseeds, toasted and ground into a powder** (see page 14 and cooking tip)
- 1½ cups **water,** plus more if needed
- ½ **red onion, diced** (1 cup)
- ½ teaspoon **salt**
- ¼ cup *Ye'qimem Zeyet* (page 25)
- 2 tablespoons **unsalted tomato paste**
- 6 cloves **garlic, pressed or grated** (1 tablespoon)
- ¼ teaspoon *Ye'wot Qimem* (page 40; optional)
- 3 tablespoons **ground *berbere*** (see page 21)
- ½ **jalapeño chile, sliced into ¼-inch rounds** (optional)

Put the toasted flax powder in a medium bowl. Add the water and whisk to combine. Set aside to thicken, whisking the mixture occasionally.

Put the onion and salt in a medium, dry saucepan. Cover and cook over medium-high heat, stirring occasionally to prevent sticking and burning, until the onion has released its liquid and softened, about 5 minutes. Add the *Ye'qimem Zeyet* and stir to combine. Cover and cook, stirring frequently, until the onion is very soft and beginning to brown, about 5 minutes.

Decrease the heat to medium and stir in the tomato paste, garlic, and optional *Ye'wot Qimem*. Cook uncovered, stirring frequently, until the garlic and spices no longer taste raw and the mixture forms a thick sauce, about 5 minutes. Stir in the *berbere*. Quickly stir in the flaxseed mixture. Increase the heat to high and bring to a boil. Decrease the heat to medium and simmer gently, stirring frequently, until the sauce has thickened to the consistency of pancake batter and the oil has separated and glistens on the top, about 15 minutes. If the sauce is too thick, add up to ½ cup more water to thin it. Season to taste with additional salt if desired. Top with the optional chile.

Per cup: 541 calories, 7 g protein, 51 g fat (2 g sat), 23 g carbohydrates, 303 mg sodium, 138 mg calcium, 98 g fiber

Note: Because store-bought berbere spice will vary in ingredients, sodium levels may vary.

COOKING TIP: Toasting flaxseeds takes a little practice, so pay close attention and don't walk away from the stove. If the seeds aren't sufficiently toasted, the *wot* won't have the deep-roasted flavor that's essential to this dish, but if the flaxseeds burn, the dish will taste bitter.

STORAGE TIP: Toasted flaxseeds don't store well because their oil goes rancid quickly, so be sure to cook this *wot* the same day you toast and grind the seeds. Eat it promptly too, because unlike other *wot*, this will only keep for a couple of days in the fridge.

Ye'telba Firfir (*injera* in a spicy flaxseed sauce): Put a portion of *wot* in a medium saucepan and heat over medium-low heat until hot. Add about twice as much chopped or torn *injera* as *wot* and cook, stirring frequently, until the *injera* has absorbed the sauce and softened and is heated through.

n this recipe, I walk you through the steps of making a basic *kay wot* sauce, or *kulet* (see page 68), which you can then use in whatever way you like. However, I suggest making one of the other recipes in this chapter before attempting this one, since they offer a little more guidance.

kulet

A BASIC, EASILY CUSTOMIZABLE, SPICY RED SAUCE

MAKES 6 CUPS

See photo facing page 90

1½ **small red onion, minced** (2 cups)

½ teaspoon **salt,** plus more if desired

2 tablespoons **Ye'qimem Zeyet** (page 25) **or extra-virgin olive oil**

1 **small tomato, diced** (¾ cup)

6 cloves **garlic, pressed or grated** (1 tablespoon)

2 teaspoons **peeled and grated fresh ginger**

½ teaspoon **Ye'wot Qimem** (page 40; optional)

3 tablespoons **ground *berbere*** (see page 21) **or *Berbere* Paste** (page 22)

1 tablespoon **mild paprika**

1 teaspoon **ground coriander**

⅛ teaspoon **ground cardamom**

   Pinch **ground cloves**

6 cups **chopped vegetables, veggie protein, or a combination** (see page 91)

1½ cups **water or Sleepy Vegetable Stock** (page 38), plus more if needed (see cooking tip)

Put the onion and salt in a large, dry saucepan. Cover and cook over medium-high heat, stirring occasionally to prevent sticking or burning, until the onion has released its liquid and softened, about 5 minutes. Decrease the heat to medium, add the *Ye'qimem Zeyet*, and stir to combine, scraping up any onion that has stuck to the bottom of the pan. Cover and cook, stirring occasionally, until the onion is very soft and is beginning to brown, about 10 minutes. If the onion is sticking or burning, decrease the heat slightly.

Add the tomato, garlic, ginger, and optional *Ye'wot Qimem* and stir to combine. Cover and cook, stirring frequently, until the tomato is soft but still chunky, about 5 minutes. Add the *berbere*, paprika, coriander, cardamom, and cloves and stir well to combine. Add the chopped vegetables and water. Increase the heat to high and bring to a boil. Decrease the heat to medium, cover, and simmer, stirring frequently, until the vegetables are tender, about 20 minutes. Add up to ½ cup of additional water if needed to thin the sauce.

Per 1 cup: 145 calories, 3 g protein, 6 g fat (1 g sat), 14 g carbohydrates, 712 mg sodium, 56 mg calcium, 5 g fiber

Note: Because store-bought berbere spice will vary in ingredients, sodium levels may vary. Analysis is based on using 6 cups of chopped vegetables.

Clockwise from top: **Ayib Be'gomen**, *page 124;* **Ye'telba Wot**, *page 88;* **Ye'souf Fitfit**, *page 149;* **Kulet with Ye'shimbra Duket Kwas, carrot fingers, and green beans**, *pages 90 and 162;* **Ye'siquar Denich Atakilt**, *page 136 variation*

Clockwise from top: **Ye'ater kik wot,** *page 73 variation;* **Ethiopian style mac 'n' cheesie,** *page 126;* **Ye'bedergan wot,** *page 82;*
Ye'atakilt alicha, *page 100;* **Ye'ater kik wot,** *page 73 variation;* **Ethiopian style mac 'n' cheesie,** *page 126;*
Ethiopian-style roasted Brussels sprouts, *page 125;* **Ye'atakilt alicha,** *page 100; center:* **Selata,** *page 132*

Vegetable and Veggie Protein Suggestions

- *Ye'tshom Kwalima Kwas* (page 159), *Ye'tofu Kwas* (page 160), or *Ye'shimbra Duket Kwas* (page 162)
- Beans: cooked or canned white beans or black-eyed peas
- Pan-fried jackfruit (brined and canned)
- Vegetables: artichoke hearts, beets, carrots, cauliflower, carrots, collard greens, green beans, kale, mushrooms, potatoes, rutabaga, sweet potatoes, turnips, winter squash, zucchini
- Pan-fried tempeh, baked tofu, or Seasoned Gluten (page 164)

COOKING TIP: Feel free to experiment with the liquid in this recipe by replacing ½ cup of the water or stock with beer or wine. The texture of the finished dish depends on the vegetables and plant protein you add, but the *kulet* will have the consistency of a slightly chunky marinara. Add quick-cooking vegetables toward the end of the cooking time so they don't overcook.

SERVING SUGGESTIONS

If you make this *kulet* on the spicier side, pair it with a cooling dish, such as *Butecha* (page 139), *Ye'ater Kik Alicha* (page 96), *Ayib* (page 36), or lightly salted chunks of avocado.

f you're not a fan of okra but wish you were, this stew is for you. For ease, use frozen okra, and let the dumplings sit in the gravy long enough to soak it up and soften.

ye'tofu kwas wot be'bamya

TENDER OKRA AND DUMPLINGS IN A SPICY SAUCE

MAKES 4 CUPS

½ **red onion, minced** (1 cup)

½ teaspoon **salt,** plus more if desired

2 tablespoons **Ye'qimem Zeyet** (page 25) **or extra-virgin olive oil**

6 cloves **garlic, pressed or grated** (1 tablespoon)

1 tablespoon **unsalted tomato paste**

1 teaspoon **ground cumin**

¼ teaspoon **Ye'wot Qimem** (page 40; optional)

3 tablespoons **ground *berbere*** (see page 21) **or *Berbere* Paste** (page 22)

1 tablespoon **mild paprika**

2 cups **water or Sleepy Vegetable Stock** (page 38)

2 cups **sliced fresh or frozen okra,** in ½-inch segments

20 **Ye'tofu Kwas** (page 160), **Ye'tshom Kwalima Kwas** (page 159), **or Ye'shimbra Duket Kwas** (page 162)

   Freshly ground black pepper

¼ cup **minced green onion**

Put the red onion and salt in a large, dry saucepan. Cover and cook over medium-high heat, stirring occasionally to prevent sticking and burning, until the onion has released its liquid and softened, about 5 minutes. Decrease the heat to medium. Add the *Ye'qimem Zeyet* and stir to combine, scraping up any onion that has stuck to the bottom of the pan. Cover and cook, stirring occasionally, until the onion is very soft and beginning to brown, about 10 minutes. If the onion sticks or begins to burn, decrease the heat slightly.

Add the garlic, tomato paste, cumin, and optional *Ye'wot Qimem* and cook uncovered, stirring frequently, for 5 minutes. Stir in the *berbere* and paprika and mix well. Add the water and okra. Increase the heat to high and bring to a boil. Decrease the heat to medium, cover, and simmer, stirring frequently, until the sauce has thickened slightly and the okra is tender, about 15 minutes.

Arrange the *Ye'tofu Kwas* in a single layer in the stew, ladling the sauce over the top of each one. Cover and simmer gently until heated through, about 5 minutes. Season to taste with pepper and additional salt if desired. Sprinkle the green onion over the top.

Per cup: 405 calories, 25 g protein, 17 g fat (2 g sat), 39 g carbohydrates, 494 mg sodium, 252 mg calcium, 13 g fiber

Note: Because store-bought berbere spice will vary in ingredients, sodium levels may vary.

In this chapter, I've gathered all the information and recipes you need to make your own beautiful, golden *alicha wot*. Unlike spicy *kay wot*, *alicha wot* can be quite mild (although they can also have a fiery bite from hot green chiles). This style of *wot* is generally seasoned with turmeric, garlic, ginger, and green chiles. They are often referred to as "Ethiopian curry," and you can recognize them by their golden turmeric glow, mild ginger-garlic flavor, and green chile punctuation.

6 alicha wot
MILD GOLDEN SAUCES AND STEWS

Basic *Alicha Wot* Steps

aking *alicha wot* is a bit less structured than making *kay wot*. Here is the general method:

1. Finely minced white or yellow onion is cooked with salt and *Ye'qimem Zeyet* (page 25) until the onion softens and turns translucent (try not to let the onion brown too much).

3. Seasonings are added: spices, garlic, ginger, and sometimes tomatoes.

4. Water, stock, or alcohol is added and the mixture is brought to a boil. The heat is decreased and the mixture is simmered until the onion has broken down into the liquid.

5. The main ingredient is added and the stew is cooked until the flavors are well combined and the sauce has reduced and thickened.

6. A few minutes before serving, green chile is added so it can soften and lightly flavor the dish.

7. The *alicha wot* is seasoned to taste and then served warm or hot with *injera*.

A NOTE ABOUT *ALICHA WOT* INGREDIENTS

Onion

For a prettier final dish, white or yellow onion is generally used because of its neutral color. If you don't mind bits of onion showing through, use red if that's what you have on hand; it won't make much difference in terms of the taste. Even though the onion isn't cooked down quite as much as it is in *kay wot*, it's still best if it's minced quite finely. If you use a food processor, remember to decrease the amount the recipe calls for by a smidge, as the amounts called for in each recipe are based on hand-minced onion: 1 medium onion, minced by hand = 2 cups; 1 medium onion, machine processed = 1½ cup.

Jalapeño Chile

One or two medium-sized jalapeño chiles (veined and seeded) add the tiniest amount of heat to a saucepan of *alicha wot*, and I find this to be perfect. But jalapeño chiles can be fickle little fellas; sometimes they're hella-hella hot, even after they've been veined and seeded, and sometimes they're so mild you can pop an entire one in your mouth without batting an eye. I've learned to taste each jalapeño as I'm working with it so I know exactly what sort of creature it is. I recommend you do the same, and if you love heat, add as many as you like. Or up the game and choose a serrano or even hotter chile. If heat isn't really your thing, you can just leave the chile out, although I'd recommend choosing something milder, such as an Anaheim chile, instead of abstaining altogether.

Booze It Up

Once you've made a few *alicha wot* and feel that you've earned your merit badge, go ahead and experiment. Try replacing up to ½ cup of the water or broth with white table wine or a light lager beer.

Salt

In order to adjust for salt variances in different oil bases (plain oil versus commercial vegan butters) in *Ye'qimem Zeyet*, these recipes have all been developed with the least amount of salt. Please adjust the salt of each finished *wot* to taste.

POINTS TO KEEP IN MIND

One mistake many people make when learning to cook *wot* is not adding enough liquid, especially to dishes that contain beans, lentils, or split peas. The legume-based stews should be loose enough that they spread a little when spooned onto *injera*, and the other *alicha wot* should have a sauce or gravy that soaks into the *injera*. Don't be afraid to add extra liquid as necessary to thin the consistency of a dish. If you add too much liquid, there are a few tricks you can use to thicken it up again:

1. Increase the heat so the *wot* cooks at a rapid simmer, but don't step away from the stove because the *wot* could quickly scorch.
2. Take the saucepan off the heat and cover it. Let the *wot* rest for 5 to 10 minutes; you'll probably be surprised at how quickly it thickens.
3. Refrigerate the *wot* and reheat it after it's been thoroughly chilled.

SERVING AND SCOOPING

Alicha wot can be served hot, warm, or room temperature, with fresh *injera* and a variety of other dishes. *Alicha wot* do a good job of tempering spicier dishes, and since many tend to be a little heavy, they also benefit from the company of a refreshing and astringent salad.

LEFTOVERS

Alicha wot make terrific leftovers and in many instances are even better the next day. Store them in tightly closed containers in the fridge for up to five days. They'll thicken once they're cold, so be sure to stir in a little water before you reheat them either on the stove top or in the microwave. If you have lots of extras, use them as a filling for crunchy, stuffed *sambusas* (pages 60 and 62), and dip them into a spicy sauce.

A long with *Ye'misser Wot* (page 72), this is a popular stew that you'll find on the menu of Ethiopian restaurants the world over. It's mild, creamy, and comforting, which means it's a good choice to serve with an array of dishes, although it also pairs well with just a simple green salad. If basil is in season where you live, definitely add a few fresh leaves; otherwise, you can simply leave them out.

ye'ater kik alicha

SPLIT PEAS IN A MILD SAUCE

MAKES 3½ CUPS

See photos facing pages 123 and 154

- 1 cup **dried yellow or green split peas**
- 6 cups **water**
- ¼ **yellow or white onion, minced** (½ cup)
- 3 tablespoons ***Ye'qimem Zeyet*** (page 25) **or extra-virgin olive oil**
- ½ teaspoon **salt,** plus more if desired
- 6 cloves **garlic, pressed or grated** (1 tablespoon)
- 2 teaspoons **peeled and grated fresh ginger**
- 6 **fresh basil leaves** (optional)
- ½ teaspoon **ground turmeric**
- 1½ cups **reserved cooking water or Sleepy Vegetable Stock** (page 38), plus more if needed
- 2 **jalapeño chiles, seeded, veined, and quartered lengthwise**

Put the split peas and water in a large saucepan and bring to a boil over high heat. Decrease the heat to medium and simmer uncovered, skimming off any foam that forms with a large spoon. Cook, stirring occasionally, until tender but firm, 20 to 30 minutes. Drain the split peas and reserve 2 cups of the cooking water.

Put the onion, *Ye'qimem Zeyet*, and salt in a large saucepan and cook over medium heat until soft and translucent (don't let the onion brown), about 7 minutes. Add the garlic, ginger, optional basil, and turmeric and cook, stirring almost constantly, for 3 minutes.

Stir in the split peas and 1½ cups of the reserved cooking water. Increase the heat to high and bring to a boil. Decrease the heat to medium and simmer, stirring frequently to prevent sticking or burning, until the split peas are soft and the liquid has reduced and thickened, 25 to 30 minutes. If the mixture is too thick, add up to ½ cup more of the reserved cooking water as needed to thin. The stew is done when the split peas are soft and tender but still hold their shape and the liquid has thickened, creating a soft, creamy purée. Stir in the chiles and cook for 5 minutes longer. Season to taste with additional salt if desired and discard the basil leaves before serving.

Per ½ cup: 126 calories, 6 g protein, 6 g fat (1 g sat), 19 g carbohydrates, 93 mg sodium, 16 mg calcium, 7 g fiber

Ye'ater Kik Be'gomen Alicha (split peas and spinach in a mild sauce): Add 2 to 3 cups of chopped baby spinach leaves along with the chiles and stir until wilted.

This dish is similar to the iconic *Ye'ater Kik Alicha* (page 96), a mild stew made with split peas, but this version is made with creamy, soft, white cannellini beans instead. When finished, this dish should have the consistency of a saucy bean chili.

ye'nech bakela alicha

**CREAMY, GARLICKY WHITE BEANS
IN AN ONION-TURMERIC SAUCE**

MAKES 4 CUPS

1 **white or yellow onion, minced** (2 cups)

½ teaspoon **salt,** plus more if desired

3 tablespoons *Ye'qimem Zeyet* (page 25)

6 cloves **garlic, pressed or grated**
(1 tablespoon)

2 teaspoons **peeled and grated fresh ginger**

½ teaspoon **ground turmeric**

3 cups **cooked or canned cannellini beans
or other small white beans** (see cooking tip)

1½ cups **water or Sleepy Vegetable Stock**
(page 38), plus more if needed

2 **jalapeño chiles, seeded, veined, and cut
into thin strips**

Put the onion and salt in a large, dry saucepan. Cover and cook over medium heat, stirring frequently to prevent sticking and burning, until the onion has released its liquid and softened, about 5 minutes. Add the *Ye'qimem Zeyet* and stir well to combine. Cover and cook, stirring frequently, until the onion is quite soft and just starting to brown, about 6 minutes. Stir in the garlic, ginger, and turmeric. Cover and cook, stirring frequently, for 2 minutes.

Stir in the beans and water. Increase the heat to high and bring to a boil. Decrease the heat to medium-high, cover, and simmer, stirring frequently and mashing the beans a little with a large spoon, until the onions have begun to break down and the sauce has thickened, about 8 minutes. Add the chiles and simmer uncovered, stirring occasionally, until the liquid has reduced to a thick sauce, 4 to 6 minutes longer. If the mixture is too thick, add up to ½ cup of additional water as needed to thin. Season to taste with additional salt if desired.

Per cup: 268 calories, 12 g protein, 11 g fat (2 g sat), 32 g carbohydrates, 531 mg sodium, 106 mg calcium, 10 g fiber

COOKING TIP: The flavor and texture of dried beans cooked from scratch are best in this recipe, but in a pinch you can use two 15-ounce cans of beans. Just rinse and drain the beans before using them.

SERVING SUGGESTIONS

This *wot* is best when accompanied by a tangy salad and a spicy *kay wot* (see page 67). Both will add tasty, contrasting flavors.

f you're familiar with Indian food, you'll notice that this dish is very similar to a mild *masoor dal*. This is also one of the fastest *wot* to make because the red lentils cook so quickly. This dish might look a little thin when it's done cooking, but will thicken up as soon as it comes off the heat.

ye'misser alicha

TENDER RED LENTILS IN A MILD GARLIC-GINGER SAUCE

MAKES 4 CUPS

1 cup **dried red lentils**

5 cups **water**

¼ cup **yellow or white onion, minced** (½ cup)

2 tablespoons ***Ye'qimem Zeyet*** (page 25) **or extra-virgin olive oil**

½ teaspoon **salt**, plus more if desired

6 cloves **garlic, pressed or grated** (1 tablespoon)

2 teaspoons **peeled and grated fresh ginger**

¼ teaspoon **ground turmeric**

¼ teaspoon **ground cardamom**

2 cups **reserved lentil cooking water or Sleepy Vegetable Stock** (page 38)

2 **jalapeño chiles, seeded, veined, and quartered lengthwise**

Freshly ground black pepper

Put the lentils and water in a large saucepan and bring to a boil over high heat. Decrease the heat to medium-high and simmer, skimming off any foam that forms with a large spoon. Cook uncovered, stirring occasionally, until just soft, 8 to 10 minutes. Drain the lentils and reserve 2 cups of the cooking water.

While the lentils cook, put the onion, *Ye'qimem Zeyet*, and salt in a large saucepan. Cook over medium heat, stirring frequently, until the onion is soft and translucent (don't let the onion brown), about 7 minutes. Add the garlic, ginger, turmeric, and cardamom and cook, stirring almost constantly, for 3 minutes.

Stir in the drained lentils, the reserved lentil cooking water, and the chiles. Increase the heat to high and bring to a boil. Decrease the heat to medium and simmer uncovered, stirring frequently, until the lentils are reduced to a thick, soft purée, 15 to 20 minutes. Season to taste with pepper and additional salt if desired. If the mixture seems a little thin, cover and let rest off the heat to thicken slightly before serving, about 10 minutes.

Per cup: 259 calories, 14 g protein, 7 g fat (1 g sat), 36 g carbohydrates, 143 mg sodium, 33 mg calcium, 10 g fiber

Ye'misser Alicha Be'gomen (red lentils and spinach in a mild sauce): Just before serving, add 2 to 3 cups of chopped baby spinach leaves to the hot stew and stir until wilted.

Ye'misser Alicha Be'timatim (red lentils and tomato in a mild sauce): Add ½ cup of chopped tomato with the garlic, ginger, and spices.

ere's an easy, quick, and inexpensive *wot*. I like to cook the lentils until they're very tender and toothsome but still hold their shape. And I make sure there's plenty of sauce to soak into the *injera*. I also add lots of jalapeño chiles for heat and flavor. Even though the ingredients in this recipe are similar to *Ye'ater Kik Alicha* (page 96), the finished dish has a very different taste and texture.

ye'difin misser alicha

HEARTY LENTILS IN A FLAVORFUL GARLIC-GINGER SAUCE

MAKES 3 CUPS

See photo facing page 122

- 1 cup **dried green or brown lentils**
- 6 cups **water**
- ¼ **onion, minced** (½ cup)
- 3 tablespoons *Ye'qimem Zeyet* (page 25) **or extra-virgin olive oil**
- ½ teaspoon **salt,** plus more if desired
- 6 cloves **garlic, pressed or grated** (1 tablespoon)
- 2 teaspoons **peeled and grated fresh ginger**
- 6 **fresh basil leaves** (optional)
- ½ teaspoon **ground turmeric**
- 1½ cups **reserved lentil cooking water or Sleepy Vegetable Stock** (page 38), plus more if desired
- 1 to 2 **jalapeño chiles, seeded, veined, and sliced into thin half-moons**

Put the lentils and water in a large saucepan and bring to a boil over high heat. Stir to keep the lentils from sticking to the bottom of the pot. Decrease the heat to medium-high and simmer, skimming off and discarding any foam that forms with a large spoon. Cook uncovered, stirring occasionally, until the lentils are tender but still firm, 10 to 12 minutes. Drain the lentils and reserve 2 cups of the cooking water.

While the lentils cook, put the onion, *Ye'qimem Zeyet*, and salt in a large saucepan and cook over medium heat, stirring frequently, until soft and translucent (don't let the onion brown), about 7 minutes. Add the garlic, ginger, optional basil, and turmeric and cook, stirring almost constantly, for 3 minutes.

Stir in the drained lentils and 1½ cups of the reserved cooking water. Increase the heat to high and bring to a boil. Decrease the heat to medium and simmer uncovered, stirring frequently, until the lentils are very soft but not mushy and the liquid has reduced and thickened, 10 to 15 minutes. Add the jalapeño chiles during the last 5 minutes of cooking. If the mixture is too thick, add up to ½ cup additional lentil cooking water as needed to thin. Season to taste with additional salt if desired. Discard the basil before serving.

Per cup: 366 calories, 17 g protein, 14 g fat (2 g sat), 43 g carbohydrates, 195 mg sodium, 60 mg calcium, 20 g fiber

This recipe is a lot like *Ye'tikil Gomen Be'karot* (page 123), except it has the addition of potatoes and is cooked in the oven instead of on the stove top. The name *ye'atakilt alicha* refers to a mixed-vegetable stew, and the combo in this recipe (cabbage, potatoes, and carrots) is what you'll usually find in restaurants. When I'm cooking for a crowd, this casserole is a lifesaver, since it bakes in the oven without much babysitting and frees up the stove for other delights.

VEGGIE COMBO • CLASSIC •

ye'atakilt alicha
STEWED CABBAGE, POTATOES, AND CARROTS IN A MILD SAUCE

MAKES 4 CUPS

See photo facing page 91

- ½ **green cabbage, chopped in 1-inch pieces** (7 cups)
- ¾ pound **thin-skinned potatoes, cut into bite-sized chunks** (2 cups firmly packed)
- ¼ pound **carrots, thickly sliced** (1 cup)
- ¼ cup *Ye'qimen Zeyet* (page 25) **or extra-virgin olive oil**
- 6 cloves **garlic, pressed or grated** (1 tablespoon)
- 2 teaspoons **peeled and grated fresh ginger**
- ¾ teaspoon **salt,** plus more if desired
- ¼ teaspoon **ground cardamom**
- 2 **jalapeño chiles, seeded, veined, and quartered lengthwise**

   Freshly ground black pepper

Preheat the oven to 425 degrees F. Put the cabbage, potatoes, and carrots in a 2½-quart casserole dish and stir to combine. Add the *Ye'qimem Zeyet*, garlic, ginger, salt, and cardamom and toss well to evenly coat the vegetables.

Cover and bake for 35 minutes, stirring every 10 to 12 minutes to keep the vegetables from burning. Add the chiles and stir to combine. Bake uncovered until the potatoes are very soft and tender, about 5 minutes longer. Season to taste with pepper and additional salt if desired.

Per cup: 250 calories, 5 g protein, 14 g fat (2 g sat), 29 g carbohydrates, 265 mg sodium, 114 mg calcium, 7 g fiber

VARIATIONS: It's easy and fun to change this recipe up a bit. For different tastes, try adding or replacing some or all of the vegetables with sweet potato, chopped onion, cauliflower, green beans, or whatever veggies you most prefer.

his *alicha wot* contains creamy butternut squash and a blend of flavors typically associated with autumn. If you want to make Ethiopian food for Thanksgiving, this dish would be an excellent choice.

ye'dubba alicha
ROASTED BUTTERNUT SQUASH IN A MILD SAUCE

MAKES 3 CUPS

½ **small butternut squash, peeled and cut into 1-inch pieces** (4 cups)

½ teaspoon plus ⅛ teaspoon **salt**, plus more if desired

1½ teaspoons **extra-virgin olive oil**

½ **yellow or white onion, minced** (1 cup)

2 tablespoons *Ye'qimem Zeyet* (page 25) **or additional extra-virgin olive oil**

4 cloves **garlic, pressed or grated** (2 teaspoons)

2 teaspoons **peeled and grated fresh ginger**

¼ teaspoon **ground cinnamon**

¼ teaspoon **ground turmeric**

⅛ teaspoon **ground cardamom**

1½ cups **water or Sleepy Vegetable Stock** (page 38), plus more if needed

2 **jalapeño chiles, seeded, veined, and cut into thin strips**

Freshly ground black pepper

Preheat the oven to 425 degrees F. Line a baking sheet with parchment paper.

Put the squash in a large bowl and sprinkle with ⅛ teaspoon of the salt. Drizzle with the olive oil and toss with your hands to completely coat the squash. Arrange the squash in a single layer on the prepared baking sheet and bake for 10 minutes. Flip the squash over and bake for 10 minutes longer, or until tender and lightly brown.

Put the onion, *Ye'qimem Zeyet*, and the remaining ½ teaspoon of salt in a large saucepan. Cover and cook over medium heat, stirring frequently, until the onion is soft, about 5 minutes. Add the garlic and ginger and stir to combine. Cover and cook, stirring frequently to keep the garlic from burning, for 3 minutes.

Add the cinnamon, turmeric, cardamom, and baked squash and stir to combine. Cook for 1 minute, stirring frequently. Add the water. Increase the heat to high and bring to a boil. Decrease the heat to medium, cover, and simmer, stirring frequently, for 10 minutes. Uncover and mash a few pieces of the squash with a large spoon to thicken the sauce. Alternatively, if the sauce is too thick, add up to ½ cup more water. Decrease the heat to low, add the chiles, and simmer for 5 minutes longer. Season to taste with pepper and additional salt if desired.

Per cup: 213 calories, 3 g protein, 12 g fat (2 g sat), 30 g carbohydrates, 198 mg sodium, 106 mg calcium, 5 g fiber

COOKING TIP: If the sauce seems thin, cover the stew, remove it from the heat, and let it rest for 5 to 10 minutes.

prefer using frozen chopped okra in this recipe because it's more accessible where I live, less work, and mess-free. There's no need to even defrost it; just measure it and toss it in the pan. This okra stew is lighter than other *alicha wot*, so it's a pleasing complement to some of the heavier dishes.

ye'bamya alicha

TENDER OKRA AND TOMATO IN A MILD SAUCE

MAKES 3 CUPS

½ **yellow or white onion, cut into ¼-inch slivers and coarsely chopped** (1 cup)

2 tablespoons **Ye'qimem Zeyet** (page 25) **or extra-virgin olive oil**

½ teaspoon **salt**, plus more if desired

2 **jalapeño chiles, sliced into thin rounds**

4 cloves **garlic, thinly sliced** (3 tablespoons)

1 teaspoon **peeled and grated fresh ginger**

2 cups **sliced fresh or frozen okra, in ½-inch segments**

1 **tomato, peeled and chopped** (1 cup)

¼ teaspoon **ground turmeric**

Freshly ground black pepper

Put the onion, *Ye'qimem Zeyet*, and salt in a large skillet and cook over medium-high heat, stirring frequently, until the onion has softened, about 5 minutes. Decrease the heat to medium and add the chiles, garlic, and ginger. Cook, stirring frequently to prevent scorching, until the garlic has softened, about 3 minutes.

Increase the heat to medium-high and add the okra, tomato, and turmeric. Cook, stirring occasionally, until the okra is tender, about 10 minutes. If the mixture begins to stick, decrease the heat to medium. Season to taste with pepper and additional salt if desired.

Per cup: 144 calories, 4 g protein, 9 g fat (0 g sat), 1 g carbohydrates, 198 mg sodium, 87 mg calcium, 4 g fiber

COOKING TIP: The jalapeño chiles make this dish somewhat spicy. If you prefer your *alicha wot* milder, be sure to vein and seed the chiles before slicing them.

This is a great dish to serve with spicier *kay wot*, since the sweet beets and mild potatoes temper hotter flavors. It also adds a beautiful color contrast to any *beyaynetu*, and it will look especially gorgeous served alongside a turmeric-colored dish, such as *Ye'ater Kik Alicha* (page 96) or *Ye'tikil Gomen Be'karot* (page 123).

ye'kaysir alicha be'denich
BEETS AND POTATOES IN A MILD SAUCE

MAKES 4 CUPS

½ **onion, minced** (1 cup)

3 tablespoons **Ye'qimem Zeyet** (page 25) **or extra-virgin olive oil**

½ teaspoon **salt,** plus more if desired

½ pound **medium beets, peeled and cut into ½-inch wedges** (about 1¾ cups)

1 pound **thin-skinned potatoes, peeled and cut into ½-inch wedges** (about 3 cups)

¼ cup **water,** plus more if needed

1 to 2 **jalapeño chiles, seeded, veined, and cut into thin strips**

Freshly ground black pepper

Put the onion, *Ye'qimem Zeyet*, and salt into a large skillet and stir to combine. Cover and cook over medium-high heat, stirring often, until the onion softens and begins to brown, about 5 minutes. Add the beets and stir well to combine. Cover and cook, stirring frequently, until the beets are barely fork-tender, about 10 minutes.

Stir in the potatoes and water. Cover and cook, stirring frequently, for 15 minutes. If the vegetables start to stick or burn, add more water, 1 tablespoon at a time, as needed. Add the chiles, cover, and cook, stirring frequently, until the potatoes are very tender, about 5 minutes longer. Season to taste with pepper and additional salt if desired.

Per cup: 180 calories, 2 g protein, 11 g fat (2 g sat), 20 g carbohydrates, 188 mg sodium, 25 mg calcium, 4 g fiber

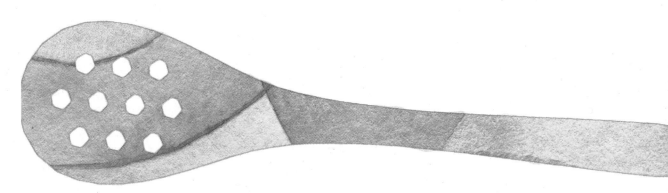

This recipe might be a little too much effort for a weeknight meal, but it also might be just what you need to swing a grumpy workweek around. If you're a good planner, make the crackers ahead of time, and since you always keep a jar of *Ye'qimem Zeyet* (page 25) waiting for your bidding in the fridge, maybe this really isn't so much work after all.

ye'shimbra asa alicha

JALAPEÑO-CHICKPEA CRACKERS IN A MILD ONION SAUCE

MAKES 5½ CUPS

chickpea crackers

1 tablespoon **organic canola oil**

2¼ cups **chickpea flour**

½ teaspoon **salt**

¼ teaspoon **ground turmeric**

⅓ cup **water**

¼ cup **extra-virgin olive oil**

1 tablespoon **veined, seeded, and minced jalapeño chile**

sauce

1½ **white or yellow onions, minced** (3 cups)

½ teaspoon **salt,** plus more if desired

¼ cup *Ye'qimem Zeyet* (page 25) **or extra-virgin olive oil**

6 cloves **pressed or grated garlic** (1 tablespoon)

1 teaspoon **peeled and grated fresh ginger**

¼ teaspoon **ground cardamom**

¼ teaspoon **ground turmeric**

2½ cups **water or Sleepy Vegetable Stock** (page 38)

1 **tomato, coarsely chopped** (1 cup)

2 **jalapeño chiles, seeded, veined, and quartered lengthwise**

To make the crackers, preheat the oven to 375 degrees F. Line a baking sheet with parchment paper and oil the parchment paper with the canola oil.

Put the chickpea flour, salt, and turmeric in a large bowl and stir well to combine. Add the water, olive oil, and chile and stir to form a thick dough. Using your hands, knead the dough directly in the bowl, incorporating in any stray flour and forming a smooth, cohesive ball.

Put a piece of parchment paper on a flat surface. Put the dough on the parchment paper, pat it into a thick disk, and roll it out ¼ inch thick. Cut the dough into hearts, fish, or whatever shapes suit your fancy using small cookie cutters.

Transfer the cutouts to the prepared baking sheet and bake for 10 minutes. Carefully turn the crackers over and bake for 8 to 10 minutes longer, until baked through, golden brown, and crispy. Let cool while you prepare the sauce.

To make the sauce, put the onions and salt in a large, dry saucepan. Cover and cook over medium heat, stirring occasionally to prevent sticking or burning, until the onions have released their liquid and softened, about 10 minutes.

Decrease the heat to medium-low, add the *Ye'qimem Zeyet*, and stir to combine, scraping up any onion that has stuck to the bottom of the pan. Cover and cook, stirring occasionally, until the onions are very soft, about 15 minutes. Add the garlic, ginger, cardamom, and turmeric and cook, stirring frequently to keep the garlic from burning, for 1 minute.

Stir in the water and tomato. Increase the heat to high and bring to a boil. Decrease the heat to medium and simmer until the sauce has reduced by about one-third its volume and the onion has cooked down and formed a sauce, 12 to 15 minutes.

Carefully submerge the crackers and chile in the sauce and simmer gently until the crackers have softened and are heated through, 10 to 15 minutes. Season to taste with additional salt if desired.

Per ½ cup: 196 calories, 5 g protein, 12 g fat (2 g sat), 17 g carbohydrates, 117 mg sodium, 22 mg calcium, 3 g fiber

COOKING TIP: If you're planning to make this dish ahead of time, be aware that the crackers will continue to soften and eventually fall apart the longer they sit in the sauce (that's one of my favorite things about this dish). If you want the crackers to be firmer and more intact, keep them separate from the sauce until serving time. Shortly before serving, heat the sauce over medium heat, adding a little water to thin it if necessary. When the sauce is simmering, carefully add the crackers and chile and simmer until the crackers have softened and are heated through, 10 to 15 minutes.

TROUBLESHOOTING

The chickpea-flour dough should be somewhat moist and easy to roll out without being crumbly or sticky. If the dough seems a bit dry or crumbly, add up to 2 tablespoons of water, 1 to 2 teaspoons at a time, until it's easier to roll out. Take care not to add too much water, since the dough should be easy to roll out without sticking. If the dough seems too wet, knead in an additional tablespoon of chickpea flour.

Dumpling *Alicha*: Replace the crackers with 20 *Ye'tofu Kwas* (page 160) or *Ye'shimbra Duket Kwas* (page 162).

like this stew best when it's made in advance and reheated; the dumplings absorb a lot of the sauce, get really soft, and break down a little. If you want the dumplings as intact as possible, serve them straight out of the oven on top of the *wot*, or add them to the sauce right before serving and cook just long enough to heat through.

ye'tofu kwas be'siquar denich alicha

SAVORY TOFU DUMPLINGS WITH SWEET POTATOES IN A MILD SAUCE

MAKES 5 CUPS

See photo facing page 155

- 1 **white or yellow onion, minced** (2 cups)
- ½ teaspoon **salt,** plus more if desired
- ¼ cup **Ye'qimem Zeyet** (page 25) **or extra-virgin olive oil**
- 6 cloves **pressed or grated garlic** (1 tablespoon)
- 1 teaspoon **peeled and grated fresh ginger**
- 1¾ cups **water or Sleepy Vegetable Stock** (page 38)
- 1½ cups **peeled and cubed sweet potatoes** (¾-inch pieces)
- ¼ teaspoon **ground turmeric**
- 20 **Ye'tofu Kwas** (page 160) **or Ye'shimbra Duket Kwas** (page 162)
- 2 **jalapeño chiles, seeded, veined, and quartered lengthwise**

Freshly ground black pepper

Put the onion and salt in a large, dry saucepan. Cover and cook over medium-high heat, stirring occasionally to prevent sticking or burning, until the onion has released its liquid and softened, about 5 minutes. Decrease the heat to medium, add the *Ye'qimem Zeyet*, and stir to combine. Cover and cook, stirring frequently, until the onion is soft and golden brown, about 10 minutes.

Increase the heat to medium-high and add the garlic and ginger. Cook for 1 minute, stirring constantly to keep the garlic from burning. Stir in the water, sweet potatoes, and turmeric. Increase the heat to high and bring to a boil. Decrease the heat to medium, cover, and simmer until the sweet potatoes are tender, about 15 minutes.

Carefully submerge the *Ye'tofu Kwas* and chiles in the sauce. Cover and simmer gently until heated through, about 10 minutes. Don't let the sauce boil or the *Ye'tofu Kwas* will fall apart. Season to taste with pepper and additional salt if desired.

Per cup: 411 calories, 17 g protein, 27 g fat (3 g sat), 27 g carbohydrates, 415 mg sodium, 134 mg calcium, 4 g fiber

VARIATION: The sweet potatoes and onion make this a rather sweet dish, and the spicy jalapeño chiles make a great contrast. For something different, switch out the sweet potato with cauliflower or another vegetable of your choice.

Alicha Firfir (*injera* in a mild sauce): Put a portion of *wot* in a medium saucepan and cook over medium heat until hot. Add about twice as much chopped or torn *injera* as *wot* and cook, stirring frequently, until the *injera* has absorbed the sauce and softened and is heated through.

Shiro powder is a finely ground spiced powder made from an assortment of cooked and dried legumes (commonly fava beans, peas, and chickpeas), and is made into a thin, gravy-like sauce with oil and water. Depending on how it's seasoned, *shiro* can be made into a *kay* or *alicha wot*. Not only is it an important staple and protein source in the Ethiopian diet, but it's also considered paramount comfort food. Basically, a bowlful of *shiro* provides your big chance to mop up as much gravy as you like with lots of soft, tangy *injera*.

7 shiro
SMOOTH LEGUME-BASED SAUCES

ook for *shiro* powder on the shelves of Ethiopian grocery stores and online specialty markets, where it's sold either highly seasoned with *berbere* and other spices or lightly seasoned without *berbere*. Lightly seasoned, mild *shiro* powder is white or blond in color and may be labeled as "white" or *nech*; it's used in *shiro alicha*. Spicy, seasoned *shiro* powder, labeled as *miten* or *kay*, is noticeably orange in color and is used in *shiro kay wot*.

Basic *Shiro* Steps

1. *Shiro* powder is blended with water or vegetable stock until smooth.
2. Chopped onion and sometimes a protein are cooked in *Ye'qimem Zeyet* (page 25) until soft and lightly brown.
3. Seasonings are added: spices, garlic, and sometimes tomatoes.
4. The blended *shiro* mixture is whisked in and slowly simmered until thickened and fully cooked.
6. The *shiro* is seasoned to taste and then served hot, warm, or cold with *injera*.

A NOTE ABOUT *SHIRO* INGREDIENTS

Onion

Don't worry about mincing onion finely for *shiro*. It should be diced rather than minced; it's okay to see the onion in the finished sauce.

Jalapeño Chile

Shiro is often served with crunchy, raw jalapeño chiles or with *Senig Karia Be'timatim* (page 143). As with other *wot*, seed the chiles if you like and use your own discretion as to how much of them to use. I like my *shiro* best when it's garnished with thin rounds of raw jalapeño.

Salt

In order to adjust for salt variances in different oil bases (plain oil versus commercial vegan butters) in *Ye'qimem Zeyet*, these recipes have all been developed with the least amount of salt. Please adjust the salt of each finished *wot* to taste.

POINTS TO KEEP IN MIND

Although *shiro* may be eaten hot, warm, or cold, and ranges from thin and watery to thick and batter-like, I prefer mine piping hot, with the consistency of a thick gravy.

1. Simmer *shiro* slowly and gently. If the heat is too high, it will splutter and could easily burn you.

2. If the *shiro* gets too thick for your taste, add a few tablespoons of water to thin it out.

3. If the *shiro* seems too thin, cover the saucepan and remove it from the heat. The *wot* will thicken in just a few short minutes.

4. Don't fret if you think your *shiro* is too thin; just toss *injera* into it and make *Ye'shiro Firfir* (page 114).

LEFTOVERS

Shiro also makes for some tasty leftovers. Store it in a tightly closed container in the fridge for up to 5 days. *Shiro* will thicken greatly when chilled, so you'll need to stir in a bit of water before you reheat it.

ozena *Shiro* has a fancy name, but it's basically just a ramped-up version of our friend *shiro*, with the addition of tomato and browned vegan meat. This version uses chickpea flour to make it easier for folks who don't have access to traditional *shiro* powder.

bozena shiro

A SPICY LEGUME SAUCE STUDDED WITH TOMATO AND VEGGIE MEAT

See photo facing page 59

½ cup **chickpea flour**

2¾ cups **water**

¼ teaspoon **ground turmeric**

2 tablespoons ***Ye'qimem Zeyet*** (see 25) **or extra-virgin olive oil**

1 cup **diced Seasoned Gluten** (page 64) **or your favorite veggie protein**

½ red **onion, diced** (¾ cup)

4 cloves **garlic, pressed or minced** (2 teaspoons)

½ teaspoon **salt,** plus more if desired

1 teaspoon **granulated onion**

½ teaspoon **ground coriander**

¼ teaspoon **ground cumin**

2 tablespoons **ground *berbere*** (see page 21) **or *Berbere* Paste** (page 22)

1 tablespoon **mild paprika**

1 **large tomato, chopped** (1½ cups)

Freshly ground black pepper

1 to 2 **jalapeño chiles, seeded, veined, and halved** (optional)

Put the chickpea flour, 2½ cups of the water, and the turmeric in a blender and process on high speed until smooth, about 10 seconds. Set aside.

Heat 1 tablespoon of the *Ye'qimem Zeyet* in a medium saucepan over high heat. When hot, add the Seasoned Gluten and cook, stirring frequently, until brown and crusty, 5 to 7 minutes. Transfer to a small plate.

In the same saucepan, put the onion, the remaining tablespoon of *Ye'qimem Zeyet*, and the garlic and salt and cook over medium heat, stirring frequently to prevent scorching, until the onion is very soft and begins to brown, about 12 minutes. Add the granulated onion, coriander, and cumin and stir constantly for 1 minute. Stir in the *berbere* and paprika.

Pour in the chickpea-flour mixture and increase the heat to high, whisking constantly. As soon as the mixture begins to bubble, decrease the heat to low; the mixture should just barely simmer. Once it has thickened to the consistency of a thin pudding, stir in the tomato and the remaining ¼ cup of water. Simmer, stirring frequently, until the mixture is the consistency of a thick gravy, 15 to 30 minutes. Add the Seasoned Gluten during the last 5 minutes of simmering so it heats through without getting soggy. Season to taste with pepper and additional salt if desired. Serve with the optional chiles on the side.

Per cup: 384 calories, 23 g protein, 16 g fat (1 g sat), 29 g carbohydrates, 299 mg sodium, 98 mg calcium, 9 g fiber

Note: Because store-bought berbere spice will vary in ingredients, sodium levels may vary.

Bozena Firfir (bozena shiro with injera): Put a portion of the *shiro* in a medium saucepan and heat over medium-low heat until hot. Add about twice as much chopped or torn *injera* as *shiro* and cook, stirring frequently, until the *injera* has absorbed the sauce and softened and is heated through.

his recipe makes a rich and decadent *shiro*. It's delicious served with a simple green salad.

ye'shiro wot be'souf

A RICH SHIRO SAUCE WITH MILK FROM TOASTED SUNFLOWER SEEDS

MAKES 3½ CUPS

sunflower seed milk

1¾ cups **shelled raw sunflower seeds**

2½ cups **water**

shiro

½ cup *miten shiro* **powder** (see page 108)

½ **red onion, diced** (1 cup)

2 tablespoons *Ye'qimem Zeyet* (page 25) **or extra-virgin olive oil**

6 cloves **garlic, pressed or grated** (1 tablespoon)

½ teaspoon **salt**, plus more if desired

1 cup **water**, plus more if needed

1 to 2 **jalapeño chiles, veined, seeded, and halved lengthwise** (optional)

To make the sunflower seed milk, put the sunflower seeds in a large skillet and toast over medium-high heat, stirring frequently, until light golden brown and fragrant, 10 to 12 minutes. Immediately remove from the heat and transfer to a food processor. Process until the seeds are pulverized and begin to release their oil, about 2 minutes, stopping occasionally to scrape down the sides and bottom of the work bowl with a rubber spatula. The seeds are sufficiently processed when they clump together slightly when pressed between your fingers. Don't overprocess the seeds or you'll end up with sunflower seed butter.

Add the water to the seeds and process for 20 seconds. Set a fine-mesh sieve over a bowl and pour the contents of the food processor into the sieve. Let the sunflower seed milk drain into the bowl. Using a metal spoon, scrape and press the seeds and pulp against the inside of the strainer. Use some pressure to extract as much milk as possible from the seeds, and scrape the thick sunflower cream that accumulates on the underside of the sieve into the bowl. This process should take 2 to 5 minutes of continuous scraping; the resulting milk will be a little thicker than other nondairy milks and very slightly gritty. Pour the milk into a measuring cup (you should have about 2½ cups). If needed, add enough water to make 3 cups. Put the sunflower milk and the *miten shiro* powder in a medium bowl and whisk well to beat out any lumps in the powder.

Put the onion, *Ye'qimem Zeyet*, garlic, and salt in a medium saucepan and cook over medium heat, stirring frequently, until the onion is very soft and begins to brown, about 12 minutes. Whisk the *shiro* mixture again and pour it into the saucepan along with the cup of water. Increase the heat to high, whisking constantly. As soon as the mixture begins to bubble, decrease the heat to low; the mixture should just barely simmer. Cook, stirring frequently, until the mixture is thick and creamy with pieces of onion mixed throughout, about 30 minutes. If the *wot* gets too thick, add up to ½ cup of additional water, 1 tablespoon at a time, to thin it. Season to taste with additional salt if desired. Serve with the optional chiles on the side.

Per ½ cup: 91 calories, 2 g protein, 6 g fat (1 g sat), 9 g carbohydrates, 113 mg sodium, 139 mg calcium, 2 g fiber

Ye'shiro Be'souf Firfir (*shiro* with sunflower seed milk and *injera*): Put a portion of the *wot* in a medium saucepan and heat over medium-low heat until hot. Add about twice as much chopped or torn *injera* as *wot* and cook, stirring frequently, until the *injera* has absorbed the sauce and softened and is heated through.

The first few times I tasted *shiro* in a restaurant, I was positive it was just puréed lentil stew. I went home and unleashed my immersion blender on a steaming pot of lentils, but something wasn't quite right. When I finally learned about *shiro*, it was a true aha moment. To keep you and your immersion blender safe, here's a basic *shiro* recipe. Remember to thin it out as much as you like.

ye'shiro wot

A SMOOTH, CREAMY SAUCE MADE FROM POWDERED LEGUMES

MAKES 2½ CUPS

2½ cups **water**, plus more if needed

¾ cup **miten or nech shiro** powder (see page 108)

½ **red onion, diced** (1 cup)

2 tablespoons **Ye'qimem Zeyet** (page 25) **or extra-virgin olive oil**

4 cloves **garlic, pressed or grated** (2 teaspoons)

½ teaspoon **salt**, plus more if desired

1 to 2 **jalapeño chiles, veined, seeded, and halved lengthwise** (optional)

Put the water and *shiro* powder in a medium bowl and whisk well to beat out any lumps in the powder.

Put the onion, *Ye'qimem Zeyet*, garlic, and salt in a medium saucepan and cook over medium heat, stirring frequently, until the onion is very soft and begins to brown, about 12 minutes.

Whisk the *shiro* mixture again and pour it into the saucepan with the onion. Increase the heat to high and whisk constantly. As soon as the mixture begins to bubble, decrease the heat to medium-high and keep whisking. Within a few minutes, it will thicken substantially to the consistency of a thick, smooth gravy. Once thickened, decrease the heat to medium-low and simmer, stirring almost constantly (be careful of hot splutters as you stir) for 10 minutes longer. If the mixture gets too thick, add up to ½ cup of additional water as needed to thin. Stir in the salt, adding more to taste if desired. Serve with the optional chiles on the side.

Per ½ cup: 123 calories, 3 g protein, 6 g fat (1 g sat), 14 g carbohydrates, 117 mg sodium, 46 mg calcium, 4 g fiber

Ye'shiro Firfir (*shiro* with *injera*): Put a portion of the *shiro* in a medium saucepan and heat over medium-low heat until hot. Add about twice as much chopped or torn *injera* as *shiro* and cook, stirring frequently, until the *injera* has absorbed the sauce and softened and is heated through.

8 cooked vegetables and casseroles

115

his chapter contains a variety of recipes for cooked vegetable dishes (*atakilt*) along with two casserole dishes that are inspired by Ethiopian flavors. Like the milder *alicha wot* (see page 93), *atakilt* follow some of the same cooking guidelines. Whether you're phobic about spices or a rabid spice junkie, be sure to adjust the chile proportions to whatever amount makes you happy. Here are some pointers to keep in mind when making these dishes.

SALT

In order to adjust for salt variances in different oil bases (plain oil versus commercial vegan butters) in *Ye'qimem Zeyet*, these recipes have all been developed with the least amount of salt. Please adjust the salt of each dish to taste.

SERVING AND SCOOPING

Unless noted otherwise, these dishes are meant to be served hot, warm, or room temperature, with fresh *injera* and a variety of other dishes. Since these vegetable mixtures are fairly mild, they do a good job of tempering spicier dishes.

LEFTOVERS

Atakilt make terrific leftovers, and many of these dishes are even better the next day. Store them in tightly closed containers in the fridge for up to 5 days. You can reheat them in a saucepan with a little water added, if necessary, or microwave them until hot.

DON'T OVERLOOK THE EASY

There are a couple of traditional vegetable dishes that are way too easy to include as recipes in this book but shouldn't be overlooked, as they make wonderful additions to any *beyaynetu*:

- Grilled corn on the cob (*beqolo tibs*) or boiled corn on the cob (*beqolo kilkil*). Cut the cobs in fairly thin wheels and toss them with *Ye'qimem Zeyet* (page 25) seasoned with *berbere* (see page 21) after they've been cooked.
- Steamed winter squash or pumpkin (*ye'dubba kilkil*).
- Steamed sweet potatoes (*ye'siquar denich kilkil*).

Don't be fooled by the simple ingredients in this dish. It packs dynamic flavor and texture.

fasolia be'karot

TENDER BRAISED GREEN BEANS WITH CARROTS AND SOFT ONION IN A GARLICKY ONION SAUCE

MAKES 3½ CUPS

¾ pound **green beans, trimmed and halved**

½ **onion, thinly sliced into half-moons** (1 cup)

2 tablespoons *Ye'qimem Zeyet* (page 25) **or extra-virgin olive oil**

½ teaspoon **salt,** plus more if desired

2 cloves **garlic, pressed or grated** (1 teaspoon)

1 **large carrot, peeled and cut into sticks** (1 cup; see page 13)

⅛ teaspoon **ground turmeric**

⅓ cup **water**

Freshly ground black pepper

Fill a large pot with water and bring to a boil over high heat. Add the green beans, decrease the heat to medium, and simmer for 5 minutes. Drain.

Put the onion, *Ye'qimem Zeyet*, and salt in a large skillet and cook over medium-high heat, stirring frequently, until the onion is softened, about 5 minutes. Add the garlic and cook, stirring constantly to keep the garlic from burning, for 1 minute. Add the green beans, carrot, and turmeric and cook, stirring frequently, for 5 minutes.

Stir in the water. Cover and simmer, stirring frequently, until the carrot and green beans are very tender, 13 to 15 minutes. Toward the end of the cooking time, the water will evaporate and the vegetables will need to be stirred more frequently. Season to taste with pepper and additional salt if desired.

Per ½ cup: 66 calories, 1 g protein, 4 g fat (1 g sat), 7 g carbohydrates, 91 mg sodium, 31 mg calcium, 3 g fiber

A popular way to make green beans, or *fasolia*, is with the addition of ginger and tomato, which creates a unique and flavorful dish.

hirut's fasolia

TENDER BRAISED GREEN BEANS WITH CARROT AND SOFT ONION IN A TANGY TOMATO-GINGER SAUCE

MAKES 3½ CUPS

See photo facing page 122

¾ pound **green beans, trimmed and halved**

½ **onion, thinly sliced into half-moons** (1 cup)

2 tablespoons **Ye'qimem Zeyet** (page 25) **or extra-virgin olive oil**

½ teaspoon **salt,** plus more if desired

2 tablespoons **unsalted tomato paste**

2 cloves **garlic, pressed or grated** (1 teaspoon)

1 teaspoon **peeled and grated fresh ginger**

1 **large carrot, peeled and cut into sticks** (1 cup; see page 13)

⅛ teaspoon **ground turmeric**

⅓ cup **water,** plus more if needed

Freshly ground black pepper

Fill a large pot with water and bring to a boil over high heat. Add the green beans, decrease the heat to medium, and simmer for 5 minutes. Drain.

Put the onion, *Ye'qimem Zeyet*, and salt in a large skillet and cook over medium-high heat, stirring frequently, until the onion is softened, about 5 minutes. Add the tomato paste, garlic, and ginger and cook, stirring constantly to keep the garlic from burning, for 1 minute. Add the green beans, carrot, and turmeric and cook, stirring frequently to prevent scorching, for 2 minutes.

Stir in the water. Cover and simmer, stirring frequently and adding up to ⅔ cup additional water, 2 to 3 tablespoons at a time, as needed to prevent scorching, until the carrots and green beans are very tender, 13 to 15 minutes. Toward the end of the cooking time, the water will evaporate and the vegetables will need to be stirred more frequently. Season to taste with pepper and additional salt if desired.

Per ½ cup: 69 calories, 2 g protein, 4 g fat (1 g sat), 8 g carbohydrates, 93 mg sodium, 31 mg calcium, 3 g fiber

At our abode, we prefer Ethiopian greens made from collards, but feel free to make them with any combination of greens you prefer. Kale, beet greens, and chard are all great options. You can even use a braising blend that's sold in bulk at the supermarket. If you want restaurant-style results, be sure to chop the greens as finely as you can.

ye'abesha gomen
TENDER STEWED COLLARD GREENS

MAKES 4 CUPS

See photo facing page 155

- 2 tablespoons **Ye'qimem Zeyet** (page 25) **or extra-virgin olive oil**
- 1 **onion, thinly sliced and cut into ¾-inch lengths** (1½ cups)
- ¼ teaspoon **salt,** plus more if desired
- 4 cloves **garlic, pressed or grated** (2 teaspoons)
- 1 teaspoon **peeled and grated fresh ginger**
- 1½ pounds **collard greens** (about 2 bunches), **washed, ribbed, and finely chopped** (10 cups)
- ½ cup **water or Sleepy Vegetable Stock** (page 38)
- **Freshly ground black pepper**

Put the *Ye'qimem Zeyet*, onion, and salt in a large saucepan and cook over medium heat, stirring frequently, until very soft and golden brown, 10 to 12 minutes. Add the garlic and ginger and cook, stirring frequently to prevent the garlic from burning, for 1 minute.

Increase the heat to high and add the collard greens and water. Stir constantly, from the bottom to the top, incorporating the onion mixture into the greens and helping the greens reach the heat so they will wilt quickly. Once the greens have wilted dramatically, after 1 to 2 minutes, decrease the heat to medium and cover. Cook, stirring frequently, until very tender, about 15 minutes. Season to taste with pepper and additional salt if desired.

Per cup: 141 calories, 6 g protein, 8 g fat (1 g sat), 15 g carbohydrates, 7 mg sodium, 40 mg calcium, 7 g fiber

Ye'zelbo Gomen (tender stewed kale): Use kale or other greens, such as chard or beet greens, instead of collards. Adjust the final cooking time to accommodate lighter, quicker-cooking greens.

Toasted flaxseeds taste completely different from their raw counterpart. When toasted, the seeds become incredibly fragrant and nutty, with an intense roasted aroma reminiscent of peanut butter. When serving these greens, don't drain off any excess sauce. Instead, ladle the greens and the nutty sauce directly onto a piece of *injera* to soak up the potlikker.

gomen be'telba

TENDER STEWED COLLARD GREENS IN A NUTTY, TOASTED FLAXSEED SAUCE

MAKES 4 CUPS

⅓ cup **whole brown flaxseeds, toasted and ground into a powder** (see page 14)

1 cup **water,** plus more if needed

2 tablespoons **Ye'qimem Zeyet** (page 25) **or extra-virgin olive oil**

½ **onion, minced** (1 cup)

½ teaspoon **dried basil**

½ teaspoon **salt,** plus more if desired

6 cloves **garlic, pressed or grated** (1 tablespoon)

1 teaspoon **peeled and grated fresh ginger**

1½ pounds **collard greens** (about 2 bunches), **washed, ribbed, and finely chopped** (10 cups)

½ **jalapeño chile, sliced into thin rounds**

Freshly ground black pepper

Put the ground flaxseeds in a small bowl with ¾ cup of the water and stir well to combine. Let rest, stirring occasionally, while the onion cooks.

Put the *Ye'qimem Zeyet*, onion, basil, and salt in a large saucepan and cook over medium heat, stirring frequently, until very soft and golden brown, 10 to 12 minutes. Add the garlic and ginger and cook, stirring frequently to prevent the garlic from burning, for 1 minute.

Increase the heat to high and add in the collard greens and the remaining ¼ cup of water. Stir constantly, from the bottom to the top, incorporating the onion mixture into the greens and helping the greens reach the heat so they will wilt quickly. Once the greens have wilted dramatically, after 1 to 2 minutes, decrease the heat to medium. Give the flaxseed mixture a quick stir. Add the flaxseed mixture to the greens and stir well to combine. Cover and cook, stirring frequently, until the greens are quite tender, about 10 minutes. Add up to ¼ cup more water, as needed, if the greens are becoming dry. Add the chile and simmer uncovered until the sauce has thickened and the greens are very tender, about 5 minutes longer. Season to taste with pepper and additional salt if desired.

Per cup: 206 calories, 8 g protein, 13 g fat (1 g sat), 19 g carbohydrates, 174 mg sodium, 432 mg calcium, 11 g fiber

COOKING TIP: Toasted flaxseeds don't store well because their oil goes rancid quickly, so be sure to cook this dish the same day you toast and grind the seeds. Eat it promptly too, because unlike other dishes, it will only keep for a couple of days in the fridge.

his is a mild kale dish with lots of flavor. It can round out heavier stews and sauces if you're cookin' up a feast. If you're not big into greens, give this one a try anyway; it might pleasantly surprise you. Or eat half and use the rest for super-yumtastic Spicy Lasagna Roll-Ups (page 130).

ye'zelbo gomen be'karot
TENDER KALE WITH CARROTS, ONION, AND MILD SPICES

MAKES 3 CUPS

2¼ cups **water,** plus more if needed

1 pound **kale (2 bunches), washed, ribbed, and coarsely chopped** (10 cups)

1 **small red onion, minced** (1½ cups)

1 **carrot, thinly sliced and cut into half-moons** (1 cup)

2 tablespoons *Ye'qimem Zeyet* (page 25) **or extra-virgin olive oil**

½ teaspoon **salt,** plus more if desired

4 cloves **garlic, pressed or grated** (2 teaspoons)

1 **jalapeño chile, seeded, veined, and quartered lengthwise**

Freshly ground black pepper

Put 2 cups of the water in a large saucepan over high heat and bring to a boil. Add the kale, cover, and decrease the heat to medium-high. Cook, stirring frequently to prevent scorching, until the greens are tender, 3 to 5 minutes. If the bottom of the pot becomes dry, add 2 to 3 tablespoons of water as needed to prevent scorching. Remove from the heat and let rest uncovered until cool enough to handle, about 10 minutes. Drain the kale in a colander and firmly squeeze out as much water as possible; the kale should not be wet.

Transfer the kale to a food processor and process until finely chopped, about 10 pulses in all. Alternatively, finely chop the kale by hand with a sharp knife.

Put the onion, carrot, *Ye'qimem Zeyet*, and salt in the same large saucepan and stir to combine. Cover and cook over medium-high heat, stirring frequently, until the onion is translucent and the carrot is just tender, about 5 minutes. Decrease the heat to medium, add the garlic, and stir to combine. Cook uncovered for 1 minute, stirring continuously to keep the garlic from burning. Add the kale, the remaining ¼ cup of water, and the chile. Stir to combine. Cover and simmer, stirring frequently, until the vegetables are tender, about 5 minutes. Season to taste with pepper and additional salt if desired.

Per cup: 212 calories, 7 g protein, 11 g fat (1 g sat), 28 g carbohydrates, 286 mg sodium, 291 mg calcium, 5 g fiber

ye'tikil gomen be'timatim

STEWED, SEASONED CABBAGE IN A GOLDEN TOMATO SAUCE

MAKES 3½ CUPS

See photo facing page 122

- ¾ **white or yellow onion, slivered and cut into ¼-inch pieces** (1 cup)
- 3 tablespoons **Ye'qimem Zeyet** (page 25) **or extra-virgin olive oil**
- 6 cloves **garlic, pressed or grated** (1 tablespoon)
- 2 teaspoons **peeled and grated fresh ginger**
- ½ teaspoon **salt,** plus more if desired
- ½ **green cabbage, cut into 1-inch pieces** (7 cups)
- 1 **tomato, cut into ¾-inch pieces** (1 cup)
- ¼ teaspoon **ground turmeric**
- 1 to 2 **jalapeño chiles, seeded, veined, and cut into thin strips**

  Freshly ground black pepper

Put the onion, *Ye'qimem Zeyet*, garlic, ginger, and salt in a large saucepan. Cook over medium heat, stirring frequently to prevent sticking or burning, until the onion is soft and translucent, about 5 minutes.

Add the cabbage, tomato, and turmeric and stir well to combine. Cover and cook, stirring frequently, for 10 minutes. Add the chiles, cover, and cook until the cabbage is very tender, about 5 minutes longer. Season to taste with pepper and additional salt if desired.

Per cup: 182 calories, 4 g protein, 12 g fat (2 g sat), 18 g carbohydrates, 198 mg sodium, 106 mg calcium, 6 g fiber

Clockwise from top: **ye'tikil gomen be'timatim,** *page 122;* **Ye'misser wot,** *page 72;* **ye'zelbo gomen be'karot,** *page 121;*
Hirut's fasolia, *page 118;* **ye'difin misser alicha,** *page 99; center:* **Selata,** *page 132*

Clockwise from top: **Ye'ater Kik Alicha,** *page 96;* **Beqolo Kilkil with seasoned oil,** *mentioned on page 116;* **Ye'tikil Gomen Be'karot,** *page 123;* **Ye'misser Wot,** *page 72;* **Ethiopian-Style Mac 'n' Cheesie,** *page 126;* **Azifa,** *page 138; center:* **Ayib,** *page 36;* **Dat'a,** *page 42*

Sweet, tender, stewed cabbage with meltingly soft carrots in a mild gingery sauce. Although the ingredients in this dish are almost identical to those in *Ye'tikil Gomen Be'timatim* (page 122), the result tastes completely different.

ye'tikil gomen be'karot

STEWED, SEASONED CABBAGE WITH TENDER CARROTS IN A GARLIC-GINGER SAUCE

MAKES 4 CUPS

See photo opposite, and facing page 155

1 **large carrot, peeled and cut into sticks** (1 cup; see page 13)

½ **white or yellow onion, thinly sliced** (1 cup)

3 tablespoons **Ye'qimem Zeyet** (page 25) **or extra-virgin olive oil**

1 tablespoon **peeled and grated fresh ginger**

4 cloves **garlic, pressed or grated** (2 teaspoons)

½ teaspoon **salt,** plus more if desired

¼ teaspoon **ground turmeric**

¼ teaspoon **ground cardamom**

⅛ teaspoon **ground cloves**

½ **green cabbage, cut into 1-inch pieces** (7 cups)

¼ cup **water**

1 to 2 **jalapeño chiles, seeded, veined, and cut into thin strips lengthwise**

Freshly ground black pepper

Put the carrot, onion, *Ye'qimem Zeyet*, ginger, garlic, and salt in a large saucepan. Cook over medium heat, stirring frequently to prevent sticking or burning, until the onion is soft and translucent, about 5 minutes.

Stir in the turmeric, cardamom, and cloves and cook for 1 minute. Add the cabbage and water and stir well to combine. Cover and cook, stirring occasionally to prevent scorching, for 10 minutes. Add the chiles, cover, and cook until the cabbage is very tender and the carrots are soft, about 5 minutes longer. Season to taste with pepper and additional salt if desired.

Per cup: 163 calories, 1 g protein, 10 g fat (1 g sat), 17 g carbohydrates, 192 mg sodium, 103 mg calcium, 5 g fiber

yib Be'gomen is a creamy and delicious way to enjoy greens. Eat this on its own or as an accompaniment to any of the spicy stews and sauces. I prefer this dish at room temperature, but it may also be served warm or cold.

ayib be'gomen

TENDER COLLARD GREENS MIXED WITH SOFT CHEESE AND SEASONED OIL

MAKES 4 CUPS

See photo facing page 90

2 cups **water,** plus more as needed

1½ pounds **collard greens** (2 bunches), **washed, ribbed, and coarsely chopped** (10 cups)

2 tablespoons **Ye'qimem Zeyet** (page 25)

¼ teaspoon **salt,** plus more if desired

½ cup **Ayib** (page 36)

Freshly ground black pepper

Put the water in a large saucepan and bring to a boil over high heat. Add the collard greens, cover, and decrease the heat to medium-high. Cook, stirring often, until the greens are tender, about 15 minutes. If the bottom of the pot becomes dry, add 2 to 3 additional tablespoons of water as needed to prevent scorching. Remove from the heat and let rest uncovered until cool enough to handle, about 10 minutes. Drain the greens in a colander over the sink and firmly squeeze out as much water as possible; the greens should not be wet.

Transfer the greens to a food processor and pulse until finely chopped, about 10 pulses in all. Alternatively, finely chop the greens by hand with a sharp knife.

Transfer the greens to a medium bowl and toss with the *Ye'qimem Zeyet* and salt. Add the *Ayib* and carefully fold it into the greens using your hands or a large spoon until just mixed. Season to taste with pepper and additional salt if desired.

Per cup: 166 calories, 7 g protein, 12 g fat (0.3 g sat), 12 g carbohydrates, 147 mg sodium, 431 mg calcium, 9 g fiber

SERVING SUGGESTIONS

For an appetizer or snack, spread *Ayib Be'gomen* over toasted *injera* (see *Katenga*, page 66) or stuff it into *Ye'difin Misser Sambusas* (page 62) instead of the lentils.

've included this recipe to demonstrate how authentic Ethiopian flavors can be incorporated into any sort of produce you might have in your fridge, and because roasted Brussels sprouts are delicious.

Ethiopian-style roasted brussels sprouts

MAKES 2½ CUPS

See photo facing page 91

1 pound **Brussels sprouts, trimmed and quartered**

2 teaspoons ***Ye'qimem Zeyet*** (page 25)

Pinch ***ajwain* seeds**

Pinch **salt,** plus more if desired

Preheat the oven to 400 degrees F. Line a baking sheet with parchment paper.

Put all the ingredients in a medium bowl and toss until the Brussels sprouts are evenly coated. Arrange the Brussels sprouts in a single layer on the prepared baking sheet, cut-side down. Bake for 18 minutes, until tender and lightly charred. Season to taste with additional salt if desired.

Per ½ cup: 62 calories, 3 g protein, 3 g fat (0 g sat), 8 g carbohydrates, 37 mg sodium, 38 mg calcium, 3 g fiber

SERVING SUGGESTIONS

Serve these Brussels sprouts as part of your favorite Ethiopian spread or with Ethiopian-Style Mac 'n' Cheesie (page 126) and *Awaze* Tofu (page 166).

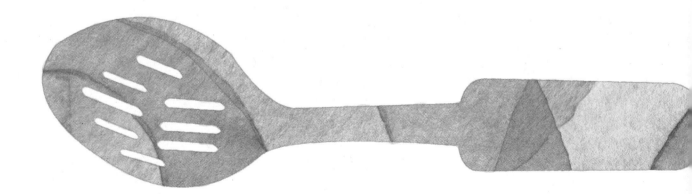

This mac recipe is a straight-up throwback to my zine *Papa Tofu Loves Ethiopian Food*. I originally wrote the recipe as an example of Ethiopian-style fusion food, but it just so happens this garlicky, sauce-laden pasta dish is always one of the first to get gobbled up when I serve it as part of an Ethiopian spread.

Ethiopian-style mac 'n' cheesie

MAKES 9 CUPS

See photos facing pages 91 and 123

1 cup **raw cashew pieces, soaked in water for 1 to 3 hours and drained** (no need to soak if you're using a high-speed blender)

3¼ cups **water**

¾ cup **nutritional yeast flakes**

1 tablespoon **ground *berbere*** (see page 21) **or *Berbere Paste*** (page 22)

1¾ teaspoons **salt,** plus more if desired

1 teaspoon **granulated onion**

¾ teaspoon **granulated garlic**

¼ teaspoon **turmeric powder**

½ cup **oat flour or sorghum flour**

2 tablespoons **chickpea flour**

3 tablespoons ***Ye'qimem Zeyet*** (page 25) **or extra-virgin olive oil**

1 pound **small pasta shells or macaroni, cooked according to the package directions and drained**

Freshly ground black pepper

Mild paprika, for garnish

Preheat the oven to 350 degrees F.

Put the cashews, water, nutritional yeast, *berbere*, salt, granulated onion, granulated garlic, and turmeric in a blender. Process until completely smooth, about 3 minutes.

Combine the oat flour and chickpea flour in a medium saucepan and toast over medium-low heat, stirring occasionally, until slightly fragrant, about 1 minute. Add the *Ye'qimem Zeyet* and stir well. Increase the heat to medium and cook the flours, stirring constantly, until they develop a light tan color similar to peanut butter, about 2 minutes.

Slowly whisk in the cashew mixture, beating vigorously until smooth. Increase the heat to medium-high and cook, whisking constantly, until the mixture forms a thick, bubbly sauce, about 5 minutes. Remove from the heat.

Combine the sauce and pasta in a 2½-quart casserole dish and stir to combine. Season to taste with pepper and additional salt if desired. Sprinkle liberally with paprika and bake uncovered for 20 minutes, until golden brown.

Per cup: 361 calories, 14 g protein, 12 g fat (2 g sat), 49 g carbohydrates, 441 mg sodium, 15 mg calcium, 4 g fiber

Note: Because store-bought berbere spice will vary in ingredients, sodium levels may vary.

COOKING TIP: Ethiopian-Style Mac 'n' Cheesie will thicken and become custardy after you bake it. For a faster, saucier version, omit the paprika and dig in as soon as the pasta and sauce have been combined. Since we can never have too much of this dish at our house (it makes great leftovers), this recipe yields a truckload of mac. If you want less, just halve the recipe and bake it in an 8-inch pan. I've heard from a respected source that the sauce also makes a great topping for steamed cauliflower.

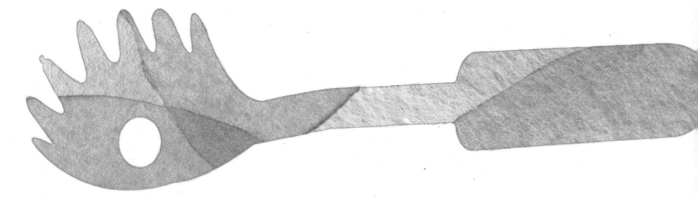

hese potatoes are a great nontraditional way to use *berbere* (see page 21) and are so delicious they often disappear before you can bat an eye.

garlic jojos

CRISPY, GARLICKY POTATO WEDGES
BAKED WITH ETHIOPIAN SPICES

MAKES 3 CUPS

1 pound **unpeeled thin-skinned potatoes, cut into wedges** (3½ cups; see cooking tip)

2 tablespoons *Ye'qimem Zeyet* (page 25) **or extra-virgin olive oil**

2 tablespoons **nutritional yeast flakes** (optional)

4 cloves **garlic, pressed or grated** (2 teaspoons)

2 teaspoons **ground *berbere*** (see page 21) **or *Berbere* Paste** (page 22)

½ teaspoon **salt,** plus more if desired

½ teaspoon **ground coriander**

2 tablespoons **potato starch**

Preheat the oven to 400 degrees F. Line a baking sheet with parchment paper.

Put the potatoes in a large bowl. Add the *Ye'qimem Zeyet*, optional nutritional yeast, garlic, *berbere*, salt, and coriander and toss until the potatoes are evenly coated. Sprinkle with the potato starch and use your hands to mix well until the potatoes are evenly and completely coated. The starch should get completely absorbed by the oil to form a thick coating; no dry starch should be visible on the potatoes.

Transfer the potatoes to the prepared baking sheet and arrange in a single layer. Bake for 20 minutes, then flip the potatoes with a spatula and bake for 10 minutes longer, until soft on the inside and golden brown and crusty on the outside.

Per cup: 117 calories, 2 g protein, 5 g fat (1 g sat), 16 g carbohydrates, 204 mg sodium, 15 mg calcium, 2 g fiber

Note: Because store-bought berbere spice will vary in ingredients, sodium levels may vary.

COOKING TIP: To cut the potatoes into wedges, first cut each one in half lengthwise. Put each half cut-side down and then cut across it laterally, angling your knife toward the center, to make narrow wedges about ½ inch thick. Alternatively, use very small baby potatoes and quarter or halve them.

SERVING SUGGESTIONS

Garlic Jojos are great for breakfast with *Ye'tofu Enkulal Firfir* (page 48), for dinner with decked out Leftover Patties (page 168), or with any meal that could benefit from a crispy-garlicky potato accompaniment. You can also just enjoy them on their own or dipped into *Awaze* (page 41).

Carrot Jojos: Replace half the potatoes with the same quantity of peeled carrots, cut into diagonal slices about ½ inch thick.

T hank you, Italy, for leaving behind your marinara when you failed to conquer Ethiopia. These roll-ups taste like you might imagine: creamy spirals of Italian-style lasagna, layered with tender greens and homemade cheese seasoned with a little bit of Ethiopian magic. The *berbere* and jalapeño chile in the *Ye'zelbo Gomen Be'karot* are a great contrast to the mild, creamy cheese, but if you want it spicier, just add more *berbere*. Serve these roll-ups piping hot with a big green salad and a fork.

spicy lasagna roll-ups

LASAGNA NOODLES STUFFED WITH SEASONED CHEESE AND KALE AND TOPPED WITH A SPICY MARINARA SAUCE

MAKES 10 ROLL-UPS

10 **lasagna noodles**

14.5 ounces **unsalted canned diced tomatoes, undrained**

8 ounces **unsalted canned tomato sauce**

1 tablespoon **extra-virgin olive oil**

2 tablespoons **nutritional yeast flakes**

1 tablespoon **ground *berbere*** (see page 21) or ***Berbere* Paste** (page 22)

¼ cup **minced fresh parsley or basil**

½ teaspoon **granulated onion**

¼ teaspoon **granulated garlic**

¼ teaspoon **salt,** plus more if desired

Pinch **freshly ground black pepper,** plus more if desired

2 cups ***Ayib*** (page 36)

1½ cups ***Ye'zelbo Gomen Be'karot*** (page 121), **dice any large pieces of jalapeño chile**

⅛ teaspoon **freshly grated nutmeg**

Preheat the oven to 375 degrees F.

Cook the lasagna noodles according to the package directions until tender but firm. Drain the noodles and arrange them in a single layer on a clean, dry tea towel while you prepare the filling.

Put the tomatoes, tomato sauce, oil, nutritional yeast, *berbere*, parsley, granulated onion, granulated garlic, salt, and pepper in a medium bowl and stir to combine. Season to taste with additional salt and pepper if desired. Spread 1 cup of the tomato sauce evenly over the bottom of an 8- or 9-inch square glass baking dish.

Put the *Ayib*, *Ye'zelbo Gomen Be'karot*, and nutmeg in a separate medium bowl and fold gently to combine. Season to taste with salt and pepper.

Spread ⅓ cup of the *Ayib* mixture evenly over the entire length of a noodle and roll the noodle into a tight coil from one end to the other. Put the roll-up seam-side down in the baking dish and repeat with the remaining noodles. The pan should have just enough room for 10 tightly arranged roll-ups.

Spoon the remaining tomato sauce on top of the roll-ups, spreading the sauce evenly and making sure the pasta is completely moistened. Bake for 25 to 35 minutes, until hot and bubbly.

Per roll-up: 200 calories, 9 g protein, 6 g fat (1 g sat), 28 g carbohydrates, 43 mg sodium, 44 mg calcium, 4 g fiber

Note: Because store-bought berbere spice will vary in ingredients, sodium levels may vary.

Whether composed of raw or cooked vegetables, the vegetable dishes in this chapter are doused in tangy, cold, astringent dressings that make them a great accompaniment and contrast to the heavier *wot* and hot vegetable dishes. Serve these vegetables cold (unless the recipe advises otherwise). All but the green salad can be stored in a tightly sealed container in the fridge for up to five days. However, I recommend adding fresh jalapeño chile just before serving, as it will lose its zip in the fridge.

cold vegetables, salads, and dressings

believe that every platter of Ethiopian food deserves at least one leafy green salad. If you're busy with other dishes, it can simply be lettuce tossed with a light dressing. But if you have the time, something a bit more complicated would surely be inviting. Cooling, crunchy raw vegetables dressed in a tangy vinaigrette are always a welcome contrast to heavier cooked dishes. While extremely basic, this recipe is a guideline for a traditional salad. But remember, the best bites are underneath where the dressing has soaked into the *injera*.

selata

A SIMPLE GREEN SALAD

MAKES AS MUCH AS YOU WANT

See photos facing pages 59, 91, 122, and 154

Romaine lettuce, torn or coarsely chopped

Tomato, cut into wedges or bite-sized chunks

Onion, thinly sliced

Jalapeño or Anaheim chile, sliced into thin rounds

Citrus Vinaigrette (page 145) **or Italian-Style Vinaigrette** (page 146)

Salt

Freshly ground pepper

Make a salad! Put as much of the lettuce, tomato, onion, and chile as you desire into a large bowl. Toss with a little vinaigrette and season to taste with salt and pepper. Serve and enjoy!

COOKING TIP: Customize it any way you like: add some avocado and sliced carrot if you want it a little fancier, and seed the chile if you want it less hot.

his tangy, crunchy slaw is a great alternative to a lettuce-based salad.

ye'tikil gomen selata

A SIMPLE SALAD OF FINELY SHREDDED DRESSED CABBAGE, TOMATO, AND JALAPEÑO CHILE

MAKES 2½ CUPS

2 cups **finely shredded cabbage**

¼ cup **chopped tomato**

1 **jalapeño chile, sliced into thin rounds**

1 tablespoon **Citrus Vinaigrette** (page 145), **Italian Style Vinaigrette** (page 146), **or** 1½ teaspoons **freshly squeezed lemon or lime juice mixed with** 1½ teaspoons **extra-virgin olive oil**

Pinch **salt,** plus more if desired

Freshly ground black pepper

Put the cabbage, tomato, and chile in a medium bowl. Add the vinaigrette and salt and toss to combine. Season to taste with pepper and additional salt if desired. Cover and refrigerate until cold.

Per ½ cup: 30 calories, 1 g protein, 1 g fat (0 g sat), 2 g carbohydrates, 7 mg sodium, 15 mg calcium, 1 g fiber

COOKING TIP: To avoid the cabbage wilting in the dressing, serve it as soon as it's chilled.

hink of this tomato salad as you would a Mexican pico de gallo. Although simple, its tart and vibrant flavors make a welcome addition to any *beyaynetu*.

ye'timatim qurt
A SIMPLE TOMATO SALAD

MAKES 2½ CUPS

See photos facing pages 59 and 155

- 2 **tomatoes, seeded and diced** (2 cups)
- ⅓ cup **minced onion**
- 1 **jalapeño chile, thinly sliced**
- 2 tablespoons **Citrus Vinaigrette** (page 145), **Italian-Style Vinaigrette** (page 146), **or** 1 tablespoon **freshly squeezed lime or lemon juice mixed with** 1 tablespoon **extra-virgin olive oil**

  Pinch **salt,** plus more if desired

  Freshly ground black pepper

Put the tomato, onion, and chile in a medium bowl. Add the vinaigrette and salt and toss to combine. Season to taste with pepper and additional salt if desired. Cover and refrigerate until just cold.

Per ½ cup: 66 calories, 2 g protein, 0 g fat (0 g sat), 6 g carbohydrates, 9 mg sodium, 10 mg calcium, 1 g fiber

SERVING SUGGESTIONS

Serve *Ye'timatim Qurt* with a combo of spicy and mild stews or with *Ye'shimbra Duket Kita* (page 50) and *Shehan Ful* (page 46).

Timatim Fitfit (tomato salad with *injera*): Add small pieces of torn *injera* to the salad and refrigerate until the bread has absorbed the dressing. Serve cold.

Timatim Qurt Be'karia (tomato and pepper salad): Decrease the tomato to 1 cup and add 1 cup seeded and diced mild green bell pepper or Anaheim chile.

his salad is a dream come true when the beets have been roasted until very soft and tender.

ye'kaysir atakilt
A SALAD OF TENDER ROASTED BEETS AND FRESH HERBS IN A CITRUS DRESSING

MAKES 3 CUPS

See photo facing page 154

1½ pounds **beets, roasted and peeled** (see page 14) **and chopped into ½-inch cubes** (3 rounded cups)

¼ cup **minced fresh basil or parsley**

4 teaspoons **extra-virgin olive oil**

4 teaspoons **freshly squeezed lime or lemon juice,** plus more if desired

Pinch **salt,** plus more if desired

Freshly ground black pepper

Put the beets and basil in a medium bowl. Add the oil, lime juice, and salt and stir to combine. Season to taste with pepper and additional lime juice and salt if desired. Cover and refrigerate until cold.

Per cup: 151 calories, 4 g protein, 6 g fat (1 g sat), 22 g carbohydrates, 199 mg sodium, 42 mg calcium, 6 g fiber

***Ye'kaysir Atakilt* with Vinaigrette:** Replace the olive oil and lime juice with 8 teaspoons of Citrus Vinaigrette (page 145) or Italian-Style Vinaigrette (page 146).

on't underestimate the delicious power of a simple potato salad. With its creamy, crunchy zing, it can dress up a platter of Ethiopian delights like nothing else. If you like more spice, add lots more chile.

ye'denich atakilt

A SIMPLE POTATO SALAD WITH RED BELL PEPPER AND ONION IN A LIME VINAIGRETTE

MAKES 3½ CUPS

See photo facing page 90

3 **thin-skinned potatoes, boiled and peeled** (see page 13 and cooking tip) **and cut into ½-inch cubes** (3 cups)

¼ cup **slivered onion, chopped into ½-inch pieces**

¼ cup **minced red bell pepper**

1 to 2 **jalapeño chiles, cut into thin rounds**

1 tablespoon **extra-virgin olive oil**

1 tablespoon **freshly squeezed lime or lemon juice**

⅛ teaspoon **salt,** plus more if desired

Freshly ground black pepper

Chopped fresh parsley or basil, for garnish

Put the potatoes, onion, bell pepper, and chiles in a medium bowl and gently stir to combine.

Put the oil, lime juice, and salt in a small bowl and stir to combine. Pour over the potato mixture and gently stir until evenly distributed. Season to taste with pepper and additional salt if desired. Cover and refrigerate until cold. Garnish with parsley.

Per ½ cup: 73 calories, 2 g protein, 2 g fat (0.3 g sat), 13 g carbohydrates, 14 mg sodium, 88 mg calcium, 1 g fiber

COOKING TIP: The trick to this salad is cooking the potatoes just right. Choose thin-skinned potatoes, which have less starch than thicker-skinned russets. Boil them in their jackets until they're just tender—a sharp knife should go all the way through easily. Drain and let them cool naturally at room temperature. The skins will come off easily.

Ye'siquar Denich Atakilt (sweet potato salad): Replace the potatoes with roasted and peeled sweet potatoes (see page 13). Omit the bell pepper and onion.

erve this bright-magenta salad at your next Ethiopian picnic party. The soft pickled beets, creamy potatoes, and sweet-tart dressing will dazzle your guests inside and out.

ye'denich be'kaysir atakilt

TENDER POTATOES WITH PICKLED BEETS AND ONION
IN A LIME VINAIGRETTE

MAKES 4 CUPS

See photo facing page 155

¼ cup **extra-virgin olive oil**

¼ cup **freshly squeezed lime or lemon juice**

1 tablespoon **whole-grain mustard**

1 teaspoon **agave nectar**

½ teaspoon **salt,** plus more if desired

8 ounces **small red beets, roasted and peeled** (see page 14) **and cut into sticks** (between ¼- and ½-inch thick)

½ cup **thinly sliced onion**

3 **thin-skinned potatoes, boiled and peeled** (see page 13 and cooking tip, page 136) and cut into ½-inch cubes (3 cups)

Freshly ground black pepper

Put the oil, lime juice, mustard, agave nectar, and salt in a medium bowl and stir well to combine. Add the beets and onion and stir gently to combine. Cover and let marinate in the refrigerator for 1 to 12 hours.

Put the potatoes in a large bowl and add the beet mixture. Stir gently to combine. Season to taste with pepper and additional salt if desired. Cover and refrigerate until cold.

Per cup: 300 calories, 4 g protein, 15 g fat (2 g sat), 38 g carbohydrates, 62 mg sodium, 37 mg calcium, 6 g fiber

love eating this salad with steamed sweet potatoes and lots of fresh basil. Usually *azifa* is seasoned with ground mustard for a little kick, but I like the zestier bite of horseradish instead. This salad tastes best when allowed to marinate in the fridge for a few hours before serving.

azifa

TANGY LENTIL SALAD

MAKES 3 CUPS

See photos facing pages 123 and 154

lentils

- 1 cup **dried brown, green, or French lentils** (see cooking tip)
- 5 cups **water**

dressing

- 2 tablespoons **extra-virgin olive oil**
- 2 tablespoons **prepared horseradish**
- 2 teaspoons **lemon zest**
- 2 tablespoons **freshly squeezed lemon juice**
- ½ teaspoon **salt,** plus more if desired
- ⅛ teaspoon **freshly ground black pepper**

salad

- ½ **tomato, diced** (½ cup)
- ⅓ cup **diced red onion**
- ¼ cup **minced fresh parsley or basil or a combination**
- 1 **jalapeño chile, seeded, veined, and minced,** plus more if desired

  Freshly ground black pepper

To cook the lentils, put the lentils and water in a large saucepan and bring to a boil over high heat. Stir to prevent the lentils from sticking to the bottom of the pan. Decrease the heat to medium and simmer uncovered, skimming off any foam that forms on the top with a large spoon. Cook, stirring occasionally, until the lentils are quite tender but not mushy, 20 to 25 minutes. Drain, discarding the cooking water, and return the lentils to the saucepan or transfer them to a medium bowl. Mash them slightly if desired (see cooking tip).

To make the dressing, combine all the dressing ingredients in a glass jar and shake well to combine.

To make the salad, add the tomato, onion, parsley, and chile to the warm lentils and stir gently to combine. Stir in the dressing and season to taste with additional salt, pepper, and chile if desired. Cover and refrigerate until cold.

Per cup: 202 calories, 13 g protein, 9 g fat (1 g sat), 32 g carbohydrates, 234 mg sodium, 33 mg calcium, 14 g fiber

COOKING TIP: I prefer *Azifa* made with French lentils, also called du Puy lentils, because I love their tiny size and the way they hold their shape when cooked. However, this salad is often served with mashed or puréed lentils, which is perfect if you accidentally overcook them. If you prefer this texture or want to try it this way, use brown or green lentils, which are softer when cooked and don't hold their shape as well as the French variety.

Azifa Fitfit (lentil salad with *injera*): Add small pieces of torn *injera* to the salad and stir to combine. Cover and refrigerate until the bread has softened and absorbed dressing.

utecha, also known as "fasting eggs" or *ye'shimbra ayib*, which means "chickpea cheese," is a bit of an enigma. It has a cult following from lucky fans who have tasted it in restaurants (it's only served in a handful of places across the United States). I've modeled this recipe after the firmer, more eggy-tasting *butecha* I've heard friends rave about. It's tangy like a salad but also creamy and cooling.

butecha

A TANGY, CREAMY SALAD OF CHICKPEA TOFU
WITH JALAPEÑO CHILE AND ONION

MAKES 2½ CUPS

See photo facing page 59

⅓ cup **minced onion**

1½ tablespoons **extra-virgin olive oil**

¼ teaspoon **salt,** plus more if desired

1 clove **garlic, pressed or grated** (1 teaspoon)

1 **jalapeño chile, seeded, veined, and minced**

2 tablespoons **freshly squeezed lemon juice**

1 (8-inch square) pan **Quick Chickpea Tofu** (page 161), **cold**

Freshly ground black pepper

Put the onion, oil, and salt in a small saucepan and cook over medium heat, stirring frequently, for 4 minutes. Add the garlic and cook, stirring constantly, until the onion is soft and golden brown, about 2 minutes. Add the chile and cook for 1 minute. Remove from the heat and stir in the lemon juice.

Just before serving, transfer the chickpea tofu to a medium bowl and mash it lightly with a fork for an eggy texture. Alternatively, dice it. Pour the onion mixture over the chickpea tofu and stir or toss to combine. Season to taste with pepper and additional salt if desired. Serve immediately or cover and refrigerate until just cold.

Per ½ cup: 144 calories, 5 g protein, 6 g fat (1 g sat), 5 g carbohydrates, 15 mg sodium, 33 mg calcium, 5 g fiber

SERVING SUGGESTIONS

Butecha is excellent paired with spicy stews and sauces. It's also a breakfast delight, by the plateful or even atop a piece of toast. I prefer my *Butecha* cold, straight out of the fridge, but it's good at room temperature too.

ere's my vegan spin on "special *kitfo*," a popular Ethiopian beef tartare dish. This version uses tender roasted beets, seasoned oil, and a rich homemade cheese to replace the traditional animal ingredients. If you love heat, add extra *Mitmita* to spice it up.

ye'kaysir kitfo be'ayib

TENDER ROASTED BEETS, MINCED AND BLENDED WITH SOFT CHEESE, SPICES, AND SEASONED OIL

MAKES 2½ CUPS

See photo facing page 58

1 pound **small red beets, roasted and peeled** (see page 14)

2 teaspoons **Ye'qimem Zeyet** (page 25) **or extra-virgin olive oil,** plus more for drizzling

¼ teaspoon **Mitmita** (page 39) **or cayenne,** plus more if desired

¼ teaspoon **ground coriander**

¼ teaspoon **salt,** plus more if desired

⅛ teaspoon **ground cardamom**

⅔ cup **Ayib** (page 36), plus an extra dollop for serving

Freshly ground black pepper

Coarsely chop the beets and put them in a food processor. Pulse in short bursts until minced, stopping frequently to scrape down the sides of the work bowl with a rubber spatula. Take care not to purée the beets.

Transfer the beets to a small bowl and add the *Ye'qimem Zeyet, Mitmita,* coriander, salt, and cardamom. Gently fold in the *Ayib* and season to taste with pepper and additional *Mitmita* and salt if desired. Top with a dollop of additional *Ayib* and a drizzle of *Ye'qimem Zeyet.*

Per ½ cup: 76 calories, 2 g protein, 4 g fat (1 g sat), 7 g carbohydrates, 285 mg sodium, 62 mg calcium, 3 g fiber

SERVING SUGGESTIONS

Beet *kitfo* should be served cold or at room temperature with a dollop of *Ayib* and a drizzle of oil on top. To turn this into a fancy appetizer, season the *Ayib* to taste with salt, black pepper, and *Mitmita,* and spread it ¾ inch thick on a small plate. Layer the seasoned minced beets on top of the *Ayib* and drizzle with extra *Ye'qimem Zeyet* and a few grinds of black pepper. Serve with crackers, bread, or toasted *injera* (page 30).

hen I was working on this book, I started tossing Quick Chickpea Tofu leftovers in salad and liked it so much, I thought I'd include a recipe. Chickpea tofu is a fast and nutritious addition to any salad, and the creamy elements of this dish are a pleasing contrast to the hearty kale.

creamy chickpea tofu and kale salad

MAKES 8 CUPS

1 bunch **kale, washed, ribbed, and chopped** (5 cups)

½ cup **cooked or canned chickpeas, rinsed and drained**

1 **tomato, diced** (1 cup)

¾ cup **cubed Quick Chickpea Tofu** (page 161), **chilled**

1 **avocado, chopped**

3 tablespoons **Lemon-Sunflower Seed Dressing** (page 142), plus more if desired

   Salt

   Freshly ground black pepper

Combine the kale, chickpeas, tomato, chickpea tofu, and avocado in a large bowl. Add the dressing and toss gently. Season to taste with salt, pepper, and up to 1 tablespoon of additional dressing if desired.

Per cup: 127 calories, 2 g protein, 10 g fat (1 g sat), 12 g carbohydrates, 43 mg sodium, 84 mg calcium, 5 g fiber

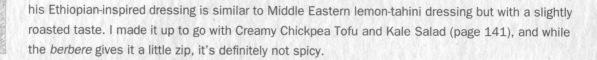

his Ethiopian-inspired dressing is similar to Middle Eastern lemon-tahini dressing but with a slightly roasted taste. I made it up to go with Creamy Chickpea Tofu and Kale Salad (page 141), and while the *berbere* gives it a little zip, it's definitely not spicy.

lemon-sunflower seed dressing

A CREAMY, ZIPPY DRESSING MADE FROM TOASTED SUNFLOWER SEEDS, GARLIC, AND LEMON JUICE

MAKES ½ CUP

½ cup **shelled raw sunflower seeds**

2 cloves **garlic, peeled and halved**

⅓ cup **water**

1 teaspoon **lemon zest**

2 tablespoons **freshly squeezed lemon juice,** plus more if desired

½ teaspoon **ground *berbere*** (see page 21; optional)

¼ teaspoon **salt**

Put the sunflower seeds and garlic in a large skillet and toast over medium-high heat, stirring almost constantly (don't walk away as both the seeds and garlic can burn quickly), until the seeds are light golden brown, about 3 minutes. Immediately remove from the heat and transfer to a food processor.

Process the sunflower seeds and garlic, stopping frequently to scrape down the sides and bottom of the work bowl with a rubber spatula, until pulverized and a butter has formed. This will take 4 to 7 minutes, depending on the strength of your machine, and will happen quickly once the seeds fully release their oil. The seeds will start sticking to the sides of the food processor, then they'll form small clumps, and then in the next instant they'll turn into seed butter.

Add the water, lemon zest, lemon juice, optional *berbere*, and salt. Process until smooth and well combined. Taste and add up to 1 tablespoon additional lemon juice if desired. Transfer to a clean glass jar. Store in the fridge for up to 1 week. Stir or shake before using.

Per 2 tablespoons: 108 calories, 4 g protein, 9 g fat (1 g sat), 5 g carbohydrates, 98 mg sodium, 27 mg calcium, 2 g fiber

Note: Because store-bought berbere spice will vary in ingredients, sodium levels may vary.

ot green chiles are a popular raw vegetable to eat with Ethiopian meals, especially *shiro*. If you're not up for fixing fancy stuffed jalapeños, simply wash a few whole chiles and scatter them artfully on top of a *beyaynetu*.

senig karia
STUFFED RAW JALAPEÑO CHILES

SENIG KARIA BE'AYIB

JALAPEÑO CHILES STUFFED WITH CHEESE

MAKES 6 CHILE HALVES

½ cup **Ayib** (page 36)

Salt

Freshly ground black pepper

Mitmita (page 39) **or cayenne**

3 **jalapeño chiles, seeded, veined, and cut in half lengthwise**

Put the *Ayib* in a small bowl. Season to taste with salt, pepper, and *Mitmita*. Mound evenly on top of the chiles.

Per ½ chile: 40 calories, 1 g protein, 1 g fat (0 g sat), 1 g carbohydrates, 44 mg sodium, 38 mg calcium, 0 g fiber

SENIG KARIA BE'TIMATIM

JALAPEÑO CHILES STUFFED WITH TOMATO AND ONION

MAKES 6 CHILE HALVES

See photo facing page 59

¼ cup **minced onion**

¼ cup **minced tomato**

1 tablespoon **extra-virgin olive oil**

Salt

Freshly ground black pepper

Mitmita (page 39) **or cayenne**

3 **jalapeño chiles, seeded, veined, and cut in half lengthwise**

Put the onion, tomato, and oil in a small bowl and stir to combine. Season to taste with salt, pepper, and *Mitmita*. Mound evenly on top of the chiles.

Per ½ chile: 30 calories, 1 g protein, 2 g fat (0.3 g sat), 2 g carbohydrates, 2 mg sodium, 6 mg calcium, 1 g fiber could eat this entire Ethiopian-inspired salad in a single sitting in a heartbeat. It's tangy, crunchy, comforting, and refreshing all at the same time.

tempeh salad

MAKES 5 CUPS

See photo facing page 26

tempeh salad

8 ounces **tempeh, steamed and cut into ¾-inch cubes** (see cooking tip)

2 **small tart apples** (such as Pink Lady or Granny Smith)**, diced** (2 cups)

2 stalks **celery, diced** (¾ cup)

3 tablespoons **minced green onion**

¾ cup **chopped fresh cilantro**

dressing

¼ cup **vegan mayonnaise**

2 teaspoons **ground *berbere*** (see page 21)

2 teaspoons **rice wine vinegar**

½ teaspoon **agave nectar**

½ teaspoon **whole celery seeds**

½ teaspoon **granulated onion**

¼ teaspoon **salt,** plus more if desired

Freshly ground black pepper

Combine all of the salad ingredients in a large bowl and toss to combine. Combine all the dressing ingredients in a small bowl or cup and stir well until blended. Pour the dressing over the tempeh mixture and toss or stir gently until evenly distributed. Season to taste with pepper and additional salt if desired. Serve immediately or cover tightly and refrigerate until cold.

Per cup: 197 calories, 10 g protein, 11 g fat (1 g sat), 14 g carbohydrates, 253 mg sodium, 71 mg calcium, 4 g fiber

Note: Because store-bought berbere spice will vary in ingredients, sodium levels may vary.

COOKING TIP: Tempeh is a cultured food that must be cooked before it's eaten. Steaming tempeh is fast, gets rid of any bitterness, and softens the tempeh, making it more receptive to dressings or marinades. Some people steam tempeh in a small amount of water, but I think this makes it soggy. Instead, steam it over boiling water, covered tightly, for 10 minutes. Let it rest until it's cool enough to handle, then chop or cut it according to the recipe directions.

This recipe makes a tangy all-purpose vinaigrette. Toss it with any food that calls for a light, peppy dressing.

citrus vinaigrette

MAKES ⅓ CUP

3 tablespoons **extra-virgin olive oil**

½ teaspoon **lemon zest**

2 tablespoons **freshly squeezed lemon juice**

2 teaspoons **whole-grain mustard**

½ teaspoon **unbleached granulated sugar**

¼ teaspoon **ground flaxseeds**

Pinch **salt**

Freshly ground black pepper

Combine all the ingredients in a clean glass jar. Seal tightly and shake to combine. Refrigerate for at least 1 hour to thicken slightly and let the flavors blend and mingle.

Per 2 tablespoons: 210 calories, 1 g protein, 21 g fat (3 g sat), 5 g carbohydrates, 26 mg sodium, 10 mg calcium, 1 g fiber

swear the secret to the delicious salads served in Ethiopian restaurants is bottled Italian dressing. Here's my homemade rendition. I've retained the components that go best with *wot* but have left out the heavier Italian herbs.

Italian vinaigrette

MAKES ⅓ CUP

3 tablespoons **extra-virgin olive oil**

2 tablespoons **red wine vinegar**

¾ teaspoon **agave nectar**

½ teaspoon **whole-grain mustard**

¼ teaspoon **dried basil**

¼ teaspoon **granulated garlic**

¼ teaspoon **granulated onion**

Pinch **salt**

Pinch **freshly ground black pepper**

Combine all the ingredients in a clean glass jar. Seal tightly and shake to combine. Refrigerate for at least 1 hour to let the flavors blend and mingle.

Per 2 tablespoons: 190 calories, 0 g protein, 20 g fat (3 g sat), 2 g carbohydrates, 37 mg sodium, 0 mg calcium, 0 g fiber.

Fitfit and _firfir_ are really fun to say but so much harder to describe. Both are made with small pieces of _injera_ mixed into plenty of sauce until the bread absorbs the sauce and softens. These dishes are very common in Ethiopia, but they're somewhat rare in Ethiopian restaurants in North America. However, if you're lucky, you might find _timatim fitfit_ or _telba fitfit_ lurking on a menu near you.

fitfit and firfir
INJERA-BASED DISHES

itfit? *Firfir*? What's the difference? *Fitfit* is served cold or at room temperature, and once the *injera* and sauce are combined, the mixture isn't heated or cooked. The sauce can be made from a variety of things, but generally it doesn't contain any *berbere*. I think *fitfit* is best described as an *injera* salad, and it's okay to eat it with a fork or spoon or scooped up with even more *injera*.

Firfir is generally eaten warm and is made with *injera* (or sometimes crusty bread) and the sauce from a *kay wot* (see page 68) or *alicha wot* (see page 94). They are then cooked together until the bread softens and breaks down. Sometimes the term *firfir* is used to describe a warm, scrambled dish, such as *Ye'tofu Enkulal Firfir* (page 48). *Firfir* is best described as a bread stuffing (think Thanksgiving) and is considered primo comfort food. It's commonly eaten for a warm breakfast with even more *injera*.

If you're not sure whether you'll enjoy these dishes, ask yourself this: Is the softened, moist *injera* that's been lying under the veggie combo and soaking up all the salad dressing and sauces one of your favorite parts of Ethiopian food? If so, you're gonna wanna *firfir* and *fitfit* all over the kitchen.

It's up to you how big to tear the *injera* pieces, as there really isn't any rule. Some people like bigger pieces, and some like smaller ones. I prefer to vary mine, with most about ¾ to 1 inch across.

In this chapter, you'll find several *fitfit* recipes, but the other *fitfit* and *firfir* recipes are scattered as variations of other recipes throughout the book. I've listed them below so you can find them easily.

e'souf Fitfit is a creamy, sauce-laden, nutty dish that reminds me of a cold, refreshing fettuccine Alfredo. It's great as a snack but also complements hot and spicy dishes.

ye'souf fitfit

TORN INJERA SOAKED IN A SEASONED SUNFLOWER SEED SAUCE

MAKES 2½ CUPS

See photo facing page 90

- 1 cup **shelled raw sunflower seeds**
- 1 cup **water**
- 2½ cups **torn or chopped** *injera*
- ¼ teaspoon **salt**, plus more if desired
- 2 tablespoons **minced red or green onion**
- 1 **jalapeño chile, sliced into thin rounds or seeded, veined, and minced**
- Pinch **freshly ground black pepper**
- Pinch **freshly grated nutmeg**
- Pinch *Mitmita* (page 39) **or cayenne**

Per ½ cup: 211 calories, 8 g protein, 15 g fat (2 g sat), 16 g carbohydrates, 125 mg sodium, 34 mg calcium, 3 g fiber

VARIATION: Instead of using this sauce for *fitfit*, serve it in a small bowl and dip toasted *injera* (see *Katenga*, page 66) directly into it.

Put the sunflower seeds in a large skillet and toast over medium-high heat, stirring almost constantly, until the seeds are light golden brown and fragrant, about 5 minutes. Immediately remove from the heat and transfer to a food processor. Process, stopping frequently to scrape down the sides and bottom of the work bowl with a rubber spatula, until the seeds are pulverized and begin to release their oil. This will take 2 to 3 minutes of continuous processing. You'll know the seeds have been processed enough when they clump together slightly when pressed between your fingers. Don't overprocess the seeds or you'll end up with sunflower seed butter.

Add the water to the seeds and process for 20 seconds. Set a fine-mesh sieve over a medium bowl and pour the contents of the food processor into the sieve. Let the sunflower seed milk drain into the bowl. Using a metal spoon, scrape and press the seeds and pulp against the inside of the strainer. Use some pressure to extract as much milk as possible from the seeds, and scrape the thick sunflower seed cream that accumulates on the underside of the sieve into the bowl. This process should take 2 to 5 minutes of continuous scraping; the resulting milk will be a little thicker than other nondairy milks and very slightly gritty. You should end up with about 1¼ cups of thick milk.

Pour the milk into a medium bowl. Add the *injera* and salt and stir well to thoroughly coat the *injera* with the milk. Add the onion and chile. Season to taste with pepper, nutmeg, *Mitmita*, and additional salt if desired and stir again. Refrigerate until the *injera* has soaked up the sauce and is cold. Toss before serving.

his fitfit contains milk made from toasted sesame seeds, which tastes quite a bit like milk made from toasted sunflower seeds, but sesame milk is a little thinner and less creamy. This dish is similar to *Ye'souf Fitfit* (page 149), but to shake things up, I've finished it a bit differently.

ye'selit fitfit

TORN INJERA SOAKED IN A SEASONED SESAME SEED SAUCE

MAKES 3 CUPS

½ cup **raw sesame seeds**

1 cup **water**

¼ **red onion, diced** (½ cup)

2 teaspoons **extra-virgin olive oil**

4 cloves **garlic, pressed or grated** (2 teaspoons)

1 teaspoon **peeled and grated fresh ginger**

¼ teaspoon **salt**, plus more if desired

½ **tomato, diced** (½ cup)

2 tablespoons **freshly squeezed lemon juice**

1 **jalapeño chile, sliced into thin rounds or seeded, veined, and minced**

2½ cups **finely torn or chopped injera**

Put the sesame seeds in a large skillet and toast over medium heat, stirring frequently, until the seeds are light golden brown and fragrant, about 10 minutes. Immediately remove the seeds from the heat and transfer to a food processor. Process, stopping frequently to scrape down the sides and bottom of the work bowl with a rubber spatula, until the seeds are pulverized and begin to release their oil. This will take 3 to 5 minutes of continuous processing. You'll know the seeds have been processed enough when they clump together slightly when pressed between your fingers. Don't overprocess the seeds or you'll end up with tahini.

Add the water and process for 30 seconds. Set a fine-mesh sieve over a medium bowl and pour the contents of the food processor into the sieve. Let the sesame seed milk drain into the bowl. Using a metal spoon, scrape and press the seeds and pulp against the inside of the strainer. Use some pressure to extract as much milk as possible from the seeds, and scrape the thick sesame seed cream that accumulates on the underside of the sieve into the bowl. This process should take about 5 minutes of continuous scraping; the resulting milk will be thin, similar to other nondairy milks, and very slightly gritty. You should end up with about ¾ to 1 cup of milk.

Put the onion, oil, garlic, ginger, and salt in a small sauce-pan and cook over medium heat, stirring frequently to keep the garlic from burning, until the onion is soft, about 7 minutes. Remove the pan from the heat and add the tomato, lemon juice, and chile. Add the onion mixture and *injera* to the sesame seed milk and stir well to thoroughly coat the *injera*. Season to taste with additional salt if desired. Refrigerate until the *injera* has soaked up the sauce and is cold. Toss before serving.

Per ½ cup: 134 calories, 4 g protein, 8 g fat (1 g sat), 14 g carbohydrates, 108 mg sodium, 130 mg calcium, 2 g fiber

SERVING SUGGESTIONS

Serve *Ye'selit Fitfit* as a snack or small meal, or pair it alongside spicier dishes for a cooling contrast.

ere's a quick *fitfit* you can make from any sort of roasted nut butter you have on hand. I like this made with dark-roasted, crunchy peanut butter, but any natural variety will do.

ye'lewuz fitfit

SMALL PIECES OF INJERA SOAKED IN A PEANUT SAUCE

MAKES 2½ CUPS

¼ cup **natural unsweetened peanut butter**

¼ teaspoon **salt,** plus more if desired

1 cup **water**

½ **jalapeño chile, seeded, veined, and sliced into thin half-moons**

2½ cups **coarsely chopped injera**

½ **tomato, chopped** (½ cup)

Minced green onion, for garnish

Put the peanut butter and salt in a medium bowl. Add 2 to 3 tablespoons of the water and stir. Add about half the remaining water and stir until the peanut butter breaks down and becomes smooth and emulsified. Add the remaining water and stir until smooth. The mixture will be thin, similar to nondairy milk. Stir in the chile. Add the *injera* and stir well until it is thoroughly coated. Stir in the tomato and season to taste with additional salt if desired. Refrigerate until the *injera* has soaked up the sauce and is cold. Toss before serving. Garnish with green onion.

Per ½ cup: 133 calories, 6 g protein, 6 g fat (1 g sat), 14 g carbohydrates, 98 mg sodium, 12 mg calcium, 2 g fiber

Telba Fitfit (*injera* in a toasted flaxseed sauce): Replace the peanut butter with ¼ cup of whole brown flaxseeds that have been toasted and ground into a powder (see page 14). Stir into the water and proceed as directed.

While *tibs* are traditionally meat-filled stir-fry dishes, ranging in heat from mild to spicy, mushroom or eggplant versions are found frequently among restaurant offerings. In this chapter you'll find two recipes for vegetable *tibs*, plus a variation that includes a gluten-based meat alternative. Serve *tibs* piping hot on *injera*, alongside other Ethiopian goodies.

tibs
STIR-FRIES

This is a quick and easy dish to make, especially if you have access to fresh rosemary. It packs a delicious punch of flavor from the fresh herb, *berbere*, and wine.

ye'ingudai awaze tibs

STIR-FRIED MUSHROOMS WITH ONION AND ROSEMARY IN A SPICY WINE SAUCE

MAKES 3 CUPS

awaze

- 2 tablespoons **table wine**
- 1 tablespoon **ground *berbere*** (see page 21) **or *Berbere* Paste** (page 22)
- 1 tablespoon **water**
- 2 teaspoons ***Ye'qimem Zeyet*** (page 25) **or extra-virgin olive oil**
- 3 cloves **garlic, pressed or minced** (1½ teaspoons)
- ¼ teaspoon **granulated onion**

mushrooms

- ½ **onion, cut into ¼-inch-thick slivers** (1 cup)
- 1 tablespoon ***Ye'qimem Zeyet*** (page 25) **or extra-virgin olive oil**
- ½ teaspoon **salt,** plus more if desired
- 1½ pounds **button mushrooms, trimmed and quartered**
- 1 tablespoon **minced fresh rosemary**

To make the *awaze*, combine all the ingredients in a small bowl.

To make the mushrooms, put a large saucepan over high heat. When hot, add the onion, *Ye'qimem Zeyet*, and salt. Cook, stirring constantly, until the onion has softened, about 2 minutes. Add the mushrooms and rosemary and cook, stirring frequently, until the mushrooms are lightly browned and have begun to soften and release their liquid, about 4 minutes. Add the *awaze* and cook, stirring almost constantly, until the mushrooms are soft and juicy and the sauce has reduced, about 2 minutes.

Per cup: 147 calories, 8 g protein, 8 g fat (1 g sat), 11 g carbohydrates, 420 mg sodium, 16 mg calcium, 3 g fiber

Note: Because store-bought berbere spice will vary in ingredients, sodium levels may vary.

Ye'tshom Awaze Tibs (gluten tibs): Replace the mushrooms with 2 cups of bite-sized pieces of Seasoned Gluten (page 164) and add an extra splash of wine to the *awaze*.

Clockwise from top: **Ye'kaysir atakilt,** *page 135;* **Ye'denich awaze tibs,** *page 155;* **Azifa,** *page 138;* **Ye'atakilt wot,** *page 71;* **Ye'ater kik alicha,** *page 96; center:* **Selata,** *page 132*

Clockwise from top: **Ye'timatim Qurt,** *page 134;* **Ayib,** *page 36;* **Ye'denich Be'kaysir Atakilt,** *page 137;* **Ye'tikil Gomen Be'karot,** *page 123;* **Ye'abesha Gomen,** *page 119;* **Ye'tofu Kwas Be'siquar Denich Alicha,** *page 106; center:* **Ye'misser Wot Be'souf,** *page 81 variation*

ere's a booze-free variation of *Ye'ingudai Awaze Tibs* (page 154) made with creamy, roasted potatoes instead of mushrooms.

ye'denich awaze tibs

STIR-FRIED ROASTED POTATOES WITH ONION AND ROSEMARY IN A SPICY WINE SAUCE

MAKES 3 CUPS

See photo facing page 154

awaze

- 3 tablespoons **water**
- 1 tablespoon **ground *berbere*** (see page 21) **or *Berbere* Paste** (page 22)
- 2 teaspoons ***Ye'qimem Zeyet*** (page 25) **or extra-virgin olive oil**
- 3 cloves **garlic, pressed or minced** (1½ teaspoons)
- ¼ teaspoon **granulated onion**

potatoes

- 1 pound **thin-skinned baby potatoes**
- 4 teaspoons ***Ye'qimem Zeyet*** (page 25) **or extra-virgin olive oil**
- ½ teaspoon **salt,** plus more if desired
- ½ **onion, cut into ¼-inch-thick slivers** (1 cup)
- 1 tablespoon **minced fresh rosemary**

  Minced green onion, for garnish

To make the *awaze*, combine all the ingredients in a small bowl and mix well.

To make the potatoes, preheat the oven to 425 degrees F. Line a rimmed baking sheet with parchment paper.

Put the potatoes in a large bowl. Add 1 teaspoon of the *Ye'qimem Zeyet* and a pinch of salt and toss until evenly distributed. Transfer the potatoes to the prepared baking sheet and bake for 25 to 30 minutes (larger potatoes will take longer), stirring occasionally, until very soft and brown. When the potatoes are cool enough to handle, cut them into quarters.

Put a large saucepan over high heat. Once the pan is hot, add the onion, the remaining tablespoon of *Ye'qimem Zeyet*, and the salt. Cook, stirring constantly, until the onion has softened, about 2 minutes. Add the potatoes and rosemary and cook, stirring frequently, until the onion is quite soft, about 2 minutes. Add the *awaze* and cook, stirring almost constantly, until the potatoes are covered in a thick sauce, about 1 minute. Season to taste with additional salt if desired. Garnish with green onion.

Per cup: 209 calories, 2 g protein, 15 g fat (2 g sat), 15 g carbohydrates, 410 mg sodium, 23 mg calcium, 1 g fiber

Note: Because store-bought berbere spice will vary in ingredients, sodium levels may vary.

Ye'denich Awaze Tibs with Wine: Replace 2 tablespoons of the water with table wine.

This *tibs* recipe is perfect for the summer when basil, tomatoes, and eggplant are plentiful. If you're not a fan of spicy-spice, decrease the amount of the chile or vein and seed it first.

ye'bedergan tibs

STIR-FRIED ROASTED EGGPLANT WITH ONION AND TOMATOES

MAKES 3 CUPS

1½ pounds **eggplant, stem removed and skin pierced several times with a fork**

½ **onion, cut into ¼-inch-thick slivers** (1 cup)

2 tablespoons **Ye'qimem Zeyet** (page 25) **or extra-virgin olive oil**

¾ teaspoon **salt,** plus more if desired

4 cloves **garlic, pressed or grated** (2 teaspoons)

1½ teaspoons **ground coriander**

¼ teaspoon **ground cumin**

¼ teaspoon **ground turmeric**

2 **jalapeño chiles, cut into thin rounds**

¼ cup **water**

1 **tomato, cut into ¾-inch wedges** (1 cup)

Freshly ground black pepper

¼ cup **minced fresh basil or parsley,** for garnish

Preheat the oven to 425 degrees F. Line a baking sheet with parchment paper.

Put the whole eggplant on the prepared baking sheet and bake for 30 to 40 minutes, flipping it several times to promote even baking, until it's collapsed and very soft. Remove from the oven and let rest until cool enough to handle. Cut the eggplant in half laterally and remove and discard the skin (it should slip off easily). Chop the eggplant into 1-inch pieces.

Put the onion, *Ye'qimem Zeyet*, and salt in a large saucepan. Cook over medium-high heat, stirring frequently, until the onion has softened, about 5 minutes. Add the garlic, coriander, cumin, turmeric, and eggplant and stir to combine. Cook, stirring frequently to keep the garlic from burning, about 2 minutes. Add the chiles and water and simmer, stirring frequently, for 5 minutes.

Increase the heat to high and add the tomato. Cook, stirring frequently, until the tomato has softened but is still intact, about 2½ minutes. Season to taste with pepper and additional salt if desired. Garnish with the basil.

Per cup: 160 calories, 4 g protein, 10 g fat (1 g sat), 18 g carbohydrates, 289 mg sodium, 49 mg calcium, 9 g fiber

12 dumplings and veggie proteins

created the dumpling recipes in this chapter specifically for plunking into wot, since I adore the way they soften and absorb whatever sauce you throw 'em into. They'll hold their shape best if you give them time to set up in the fridge for a few hours, and they'll heat up quickly in any slow-simmering sauce. The dumplings can also be enjoyed hot on top of wot, if you want them to hold their shape a bit more, or served as hot appetizers by themselves or with a dipping sauce.

Even though nearly all the other recipes in this book are gluten-free, I've chosen to include a gluten-based recipe as an option for soy-free folks and for those who aren't sensitive to gluten. This recipe is lightly seasoned to be compatible with Ethiopian flavors, and the soft, slow-cooked onion and chickpea flour help give it a great texture that slices well. You'll also find a recipe for quick chickpea tofu, which is used as an ingredient in various recipes throughout the book, along with a recipe for a tofu patty that's a great way to use up leftovers.

These dumplings have crusty tops and bottoms and are a bit sturdier than the other dumplings. Use the smallest white beans you can find, and mix them into the dough whole rather than mashing them.

ye'tshom kwalima kwas

WHITE-BEAN SAUSAGE DUMPLINGS

MAKES 15 DUMPLINGS

1 cup **organic textured soy protein** (see page 7)

2 tablespoons **tapioca starch**

¾ cup **boiling water**

⅓ cup **chopped fresh parsley or basil or a combination**

¼ cup **chickpea flour**

2 tablespoons **seeded, veined, and minced jalapeño chile** (optional)

1 tablespoon **nutritional yeast flakes**

1 teaspoon **granulated onion**

¾ teaspoon **salt,** plus more if desired

½ teaspoon **ground coriander**

¼ teaspoon **granulated garlic**

¼ teaspoon **unbleached granulated sugar**

⅛ teaspoon **ground cinnamon** (optional)

Pinch **cayenne or Mitmita** (page 39)

⅔ cup **cooked or canned white beans** (such as cannellini or great Northern beans)

2 tablespoons **organic canola oil**

Freshly ground black pepper

Put the textured soy protein and tapioca starch in a medium bowl and stir to combine. Add the boiling water and mix well. Cover and let rest for 10 minutes to hydrate the soy protein.

Add the parsley, chickpea flour, optional chile, nutritional yeast, granulated onion, salt, coriander, granulated garlic, sugar, optional cinnamon, and cayenne to the soy protein and stir well to combine. Fold in the beans. With wet hands, form the mixture into 15 small balls, about 1½ inches in diameter. If the dough starts sticking to your hands, rinse your hands without drying them and continue.

Cook the dumplings in two batches. Heat a large skillet over medium-high heat. When hot, add 1 tablespoon of the oil and arrange half the dumplings in a single layer in the skillet without crowding them. Cook until a deep golden-brown crust forms on the bottom, about 5 minutes. Flip the dumplings over with a spatula or fork and cook the other side until brown, about 5 minutes longer. Transfer to a plate and sprinkle with a pinch of pepper and additional salt if desired. Repeat with the remaining oil and dough.

Per 5 dumplings: 300 calories, 23 g protein, 10 g fat (1 g sat), 29 g carbohydrates, 289 mg sodium, 149 mg calcium, 10 g fiber

SERVING SUGGESTIONS

Besides adding these dumplings to spicy *wot* (or just poppin' them straight into your mouth), try them with spaghetti and your favorite marinara, or on a submarine sandwich with *berbere*-seasoned mayo, lettuce, and sliced tomato.

hese dumplings are slightly crunchy on the outside with a delicately seasoned, tender center.

ye'tofu kwas
TOFU DUMPLINGS

MAKES 20 DUMPLINGS

2 tablespoons **Ye'qimem Zeyet** (page 25)

14 ounces **extra-firm tofu, pressed** (see page 7)

1 tablespoon **natural unsweetened peanut butter or tahini**

1½ teaspoon **granulated onion**

1 teaspoon **ground *berbere*** (see page 21) or 2 teaspoons ***Berbere* Paste** (page 22)

¾ teaspoon **salt,** plus more if desired

½ teaspoon **ground coriander**

¼ cup **chickpea flour**

¼ cup **nutritional yeast flakes**

2 tablespoons **tapioca starch or cornstarch**

⅓ cup **minced green bell pepper, a combination of bell pepper and Anaheim chile, or seeded and veined jalapeño chile**

⅓ cup **chopped fresh parsley or basil or a combination**

Freshly ground black pepper

Preheat the oven to 375 degrees F. Line a baking sheet with parchment paper and generously oil the parchment paper with 1½ tablespoons of the *Ye'qimem Zeyet*.

Put the tofu in a large bowl and mash it with a fork until chunky. Add the peanut butter, granulated onion, *berbere*, salt, and coriander and mix well to combine. Add the chickpea flour, nutritional yeast, and tapioca starch and mix well. Stir in the green pepper and parsley until evenly distributed.

With damp hands, firmly form the mixture into 1-inch balls and arrange them on the prepared baking sheet, pressing down gently to flatten them slightly. Drizzle the remaining *Ye'qimem Zeyet* equally over each dumpling and bake for 12 to 15 minutes, until golden brown and crusty on the bottom. Carefully flip each dumpling over and bake for 10 to 12 minutes longer, or until golden brown and lightly crispy all over. Sprinkle the hot dumplings with a pinch of pepper and additional salt if desired.

Per 5 dumplings: 310 calories, 19 g protein, 20 g fat (2 g sat), 14 g carbohydrates, 347 mg sodium, 119 mg calcium, 3 g fiber

Note: Because store-bought berbere spice will vary in ingredients, sodium levels may vary.

COOKING TIP: As you mix this dough, you might think it's a little crumbly, but have faith. It will hold together beautifully once you begin forming the dumplings.

SERVING SUGGESTIONS

Try these savory dumplings in spicy *Kulet* (page 90) or milder *Ye'tofu Kwas Be'siquar Denich Alicha* (page 106), or sizzling hot with a drizzle of *Awaze* (page 41).

his chickpea tofu is speedy to make and can be used in a variety of ways. If you make this and love it, head straight over to *Ye'shimbra Duket Kwas* (page 162) and Creamy Chickpea Tofu and Kale Salad (page 141), because you're guaranteed to love those, too.

quick chickpea tofu

MAKES 1 (8-INCH SQUARE) PAN

2 cups **water**

1 cup **chickpea flour**

½ teaspoon **granulated onion**

½ teaspoon **salt**

⅛ teaspoon **ground turmeric**

Put the water, chickpea flour, granulated onion, salt, and turmeric in a blender and process on high speed until smooth, about 30 seconds. Pour into a medium saucepan and cook over medium-high heat, whisking or stirring constantly with a wooden spoon. When the mixture suddenly thickens, decrease the heat to medium and continue to whisk constantly for 5 minutes longer. As the chickpea flour cooks, it will get thick like a custard or pudding, make big bubbles that pop on the surface, and have a glossy finish (be careful of hot splutters as you stir).

Pour or spoon the mixture to an 8-inch square baking pan and let rest undisturbed for 15 minutes. It will firm up quickly as it cools. Once cool, transfer to the fridge until thoroughly cold and firm, about 1 hour. It will continue to firm up the longer it rests. If you prepare the chickpea tofu in advance, cover it tightly and store it in the fridge for up to 3 days. If any water accumulates, pour it off before using.

Per serving (based on 4 servings): 110 calories, 6 g protein, 2 g fat (0 g sat), 18 g carbohydrates, 145 mg sodium, 40 mg calcium, 5 g fiber

T hese soy-free dumplings have a crispy-chewy crust and creamy center. The first few times I made them, I couldn't stop snacking on them and ended up not having enough for their intended purpose. As a result, I rewrote the recipe with a small built-in safety net so you'll have a few extras in case the same thing happens to you.

ye'shimbra duket kwas

CHICKPEA TOFU DUMPLINGS

MAKES 25 DUMPLINGS

chickpea tofu

2½ cups **water**

1¼ cups **chickpea flour**

½ teaspoon **granulated onion**

½ teaspoon **salt**

⅛ teaspoon **ground turmeric**

To make the chickpea tofu, put the water, chickpea flour, onion, salt, and turmeric in a blender and process on high speed until smooth, about 30 seconds. Pour into a medium saucepan and cook over medium-high heat, whisking or stirring constantly with a wooden spoon. When the mixture suddenly thickens, decrease the heat to medium and continue to whisk constantly for 5 minutes longer. As the chickpea flour cooks, it will thicken like a custard or pudding, make big bubbles that pop on the surface, and have a glossy finish (be careful of hot splutters as you stir).

Pour or spoon the mixture to an 8-inch square baking pan and let rest undisturbed for 15 minutes. It will firm up quickly as it cools. Once cool, transfer to the fridge until thoroughly cold and firm, about 1 hour. It will continue to firm up the longer it rests. If you prepare the chickpea tofu in advance, cover it tightly and store it in the fridge for up to 3 days. If any water accumulates, pour it off before using.

dumplings

2 tablespoons **Ye'qimem Zeyet** (page 25)

1¼ cups **baby spinach leaves, lightly packed, sliced into thin ribbons**

½ **small carrot, coarsely grated** (¼ cup lightly packed)

2 tablespoons **minced bell pepper, Anaheim chile, or seeded and veined jalapeño chile**

½ cup **chickpea flour**

2 tablespoons **tapioca starch or cornstarch**

1 teaspoon **baking powder**

¾ teaspoon **salt**

½ teaspoon **granulated garlic**

½ teaspoon **ground coriander**

½ teaspoon **granulated onion**

To make the dumplings, preheat the oven to 375 degrees F. Line a baking pan with parchment paper and generously oil the parchment paper with 1 tablespoon of the *Ye'qimem Zeyet*. Remove the chickpea tofu from the fridge and transfer it to a large bowl. Gently mash the chickpea tofu with a fork until chunky. Add the spinach, carrot, and bell pepper and mix gently to combine. Add the chickpea flour, tapioca starch, baking powder, salt, granulated garlic, coriander, and granulated onion and mix gently.

To form and bake the dumplings, use damp hands to gently form the mixture into 1½-inch balls and arrange them on the prepared baking sheet. Drizzle the remaining tablespoon of *Ye'qimem Zeyet* over the dumplings and bake for 20 minutes, until the bottoms are golden brown. Carefully flip the dumplings and bake for 20 minutes longer, until golden brown on both sides.

Per 5 dumplings: 248 calories, 9 g protein, 10 g fat (0 g sat), 31 g carbohydrates, 223 mg sodium, 240 mg calcium, 8 g fiber

COOKING TIP: These are the most delicate of all the dumplings in this chapter. If you plan to add them to *wot*, they'll stay sturdier if you let them firm up for a few hours in the fridge first.

SERVING SUGGESTIONS

Enjoy these piping hot as a snack or in *Ye'tofu Kwas Be'siquar Denich Alicha* (page 106), or spicy *Kulet* (page 90).

seasoned gluten

WHEAT GLUTEN LIGHTLY SEASONED WITH BERBERE, SPICES, AND BUTTERY-SOFT ONION

MAKES 3 CUPS CHOPPED
(ABOUT 1 POUND)

¾ **onion, diced** (1½ cups)

2 tablespoons **extra-virgin olive oil**

¾ teaspoon **salt**

2 teaspoons **ground *berbere*** (see page 21)

1 teaspoon **mild paprika**

½ teaspoon **dried thyme or basil**

2 tablespoons **unsalted tomato paste**

1 cup **water**

¼ cup **chickpea flour**

2 tablespoons **nutritional yeast flakes**

1½ cups **vital wheat gluten** (see page 9)

Put the onion, oil, and salt in a medium skillet and cook over medium-high heat, stirring frequently, until the onion is soft, about 5 minutes. Decrease the heat to medium-low and cook, stirring occasionally, until the onion is very soft and golden brown, about 25 minutes.

Increase the heat to medium and add the *berbere*, paprika, and thyme and cook, stirring constantly, for 1 minute. Add the tomato paste and cook for 1 minute, stirring almost constantly so it doesn't stick.

Put the onion mixture, water, chickpea flour, and nutritional yeast in a blender and process until combined and almost smooth. Transfer the mixture to a large bowl and add the vital wheat gluten. Mix with a large spoon until well combined, then knead with your hands directly in the bowl until firm, about 1 minute.

Form the dough into a 4 x 5-inch log and wrap it in a double layer of foil, twisting the ends tightly (like a piece of taffy). Put the gluten in a large steamer basket and cook over boiling water for 1 hour, flipping with tongs halfway through the cooking time.

Let the gluten cool to room temperature, then remove the foil. Wrap tightly in plastic wrap and put in a ziplock bag. Refrigerate for at least 8 hours. Store in the fridge for up to 5 days or in the freezer for up to 1 month.

Per ½ cup: 210 calories, 25 g protein, 6 g fat (1 g sat), 13 g carbohydrates, 265 mg sodium, 52 mg calcium, 4 g fiber

Note: Because store-bought berbere spice will vary in ingredients, sodium levels may vary.

SERVING SUGGESTIONS

Use Seasoned Gluten in any dish that you'd normally use seitan. You can also try it in *Ye'tshom Awaze Tibs* (page 154), *Bozena Shiro* (page 110), or spicy *Kulet* (page 90).

ere's an easy, versatile tofu dish. Although it's marinated in a *berbere* sauce, it's surprisingly mild mannered.

awaze tofu

TOFU MARINATED IN A SPICY BERBERE SAUCE AND PAN FRIED OR BAKED

MAKES 8 PIECES

½ cup **Awaze** (page 41)

¼ cup **water**

14 ounces **extra-firm tofu, pressed** (see page 7) **and cut into 8 slices**

⅓ cup **nutritional yeast flakes**

⅛ teaspoon **salt,** plus more if desired

Pinch **freshly ground black pepper**

1 tablespoon **extra-virgin olive oil,** plus more if needed

Put the *Awaze* and water in an 8- or 9-inch baking pan and stir to combine. Add the tofu and pierce each slice in a few spots with the tines of a fork to help the marinade penetrate the tofu. Tilt the pan to cover each slice with the sauce, then refrigerate for 8 to 10 hours.

Just before cooking, put the nutritional yeast, salt, and pepper on a flat plate and stir to combine. Take each slice of tofu out of the marinade and hold it over the pan to let most of the excess sauce drip off. Dredge it in the seasoned nutritional yeast and gently flip it back and forth until all sides are lightly coated. Use your hands and scoop the yeast onto any hard-to-get spots. Pan fry or bake as directed below.

To pan fry, heat a nonstick skillet over medium heat. When hot, add 1 to 2 teaspoons of the oil and as many slices of tofu that will fit in a single layer without crowding. You may need to use more oil depending on the size and type of pan you use. Cook until each piece is golden brown on the bottom, about 3 minutes. Then gently flip with a fork and brown the other side. Season to taste with additional salt if desired.

To bake, preheat the oven to 400 degrees F. Line a baking sheet with parchment paper and generously oil the parchment paper. Arrange the tofu in a single layer on the prepared baking sheet without crowding and bake for 15 to 20 minutes, until each piece is golden brown on the bottom. Gently flip the tofu slices with a fork and bake for 15 minutes longer, until brown on both sides. Season to taste with additional salt if desired.

Per 2 pieces: 215 calories, 18 g protein, 13 g fat (2 g sat), 6 g carbohydrates, 53 mg sodium, 100 mg calcium, 3 g fiber

SERVING SUGGESTIONS

For a hearty Southern-style breakfast, serve this tofu alongside *Ye'beqolo Genfo* (page 52) and *Ye'abesha Gomen* (page 119). It also makes a great sandwich filling.

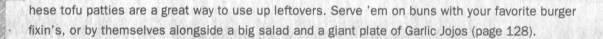

These tofu patties are a great way to use up leftovers. Serve 'em on buns with your favorite burger fixin's, or by themselves alongside a big salad and a giant plate of Garlic Jojos (page 128).

leftover patties

TOFU PATTIES WITH ETHIOPIAN VEGETABLES

MAKES 8 PATTIES

14 ounces **extra-firm tofu, rinsed**

½ cup **sorghum flour**

¼ cup **nutritional yeast flakes**

1 tablespoon **tapioca starch or cornstarch**

2 teaspoons **baking powder**

1 teaspoon **ground *berbere*** (see page 21) **or *Berbere* Paste** (page 22)

1 teaspoon **granulated onion**

¾ teaspoon **salt**

½ teaspoon **granulated garlic**

Pinch **freshly ground black pepper**

⅓ cup **minced fresh parsley, cilantro, or basil**

1 cup **leftovers from any of the *atakilt* recipes** (see cooking tip), **any large vegetable pieces diced**

Preheat the oven to 350 degrees F. Line a baking sheet with parchment paper.

Squeeze the tofu over the sink to extract as much liquid as possible, then put it in a food processor. Process until creamy. Add the sorghum flour, nutritional yeast, tapioca starch, baking powder, *berbere*, granulated onion, salt, granulated garlic, and pepper. Process until smooth and well blended. Add the parsley and pulse in three short bursts, just to combine.

Transfer the tofu mixture to a medium bowl, add the leftovers, and stir to combine. The mixture should be mostly smooth with a few small vegetable chunks throughout.

Scoop out ⅓ cup of the mixture and put it in a corner of the baking sheet. With wet hands, flatten the mixture into ½-inch-thick patties and shape into neat rounds. Repeat with the remaining mixture, leaving some space between the patties so they don't touch.

Bake until the patties are golden brown on the bottom, about 15 minutes. Flip each patty over with a spatula and bake for 10 to 12 minutes longer, until golden brown and set but still soft.

Per patty: 128 calories, 10 g protein, 4 g fat (1 g sat), 14 g carbohydrates, 236 mg sodium, 101 mg calcium, 3 g fiber

Note: Because store-bought berbere spice will vary in ingredients, sodium levels may vary. Analysis will vary based on vegetables used.

COOKING TIP: Any leftovers from the following recipes would be good to use in these patties: *Ayib Be'gomen* (page 124), *Fasolia Be'karot* (page 117), *Gomen Be'telba* (page 120), *Hirut's Fasolia* (page 118), *Ye'abesha Gomen* (page 119), *Ye'atakilt Alicha* (page 100), *Ye'atakilt Wot* (page 71), *Ye'tikil Gomen Be'karot* (page 123), *Ye'tikil Gomen Be'timatim* (page 122), or *Ye'zelbo Gomen Be'karot* (page 121).

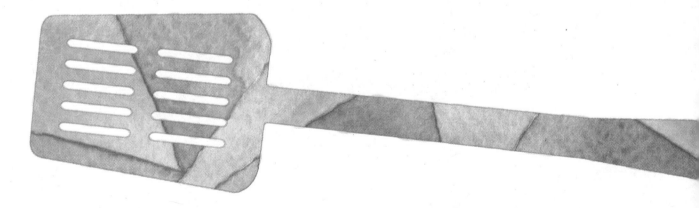

13

beverages and sweets

Dessert in Ethiopia isn't a big deal the way it is in the United States, but taking time to sit for tea and coffee is important. This chapter includes a few treats that can be eaten or imbibed after dinner or as a snack with a hot cup of Ethiopian joe or your favorite tea.

ere's a warm, spiced tea to drink while enjoying any of the snacks or sweets in this chapter. If you're not a fan of black tea, chamomile makes a delicious alternative.

shai be'qimem

BLACK TEA STEEPED WITH FRESH GINGER, SPICES, AND ORANGE RIND

MAKES 2 CUPS

3   cups **water**

2   quarter-sized slices **fresh ginger**

1   **cinnamon stick**

½   teaspoon **whole cloves**

¼   teaspoon **husked green cardamom seeds**

1   (2-inch square) piece **orange peel**

2   bags **black tea, regular or decaffeinated, or** 2½ teaspoons **loose black tea**

   Agave nectar, unbleached granulated sugar, or sweetener of your choice

Put the water in a medium saucepan and bring to a boil over high heat. Add the ginger, cinnamon stick, cloves, cardamom, and orange peel. Decrease the heat and simmer for 10 minutes.

Remove from the heat and add the tea bags. Steep for 3 minutes, strain, and pour into two mugs. Sweeten to taste with agave nectar.

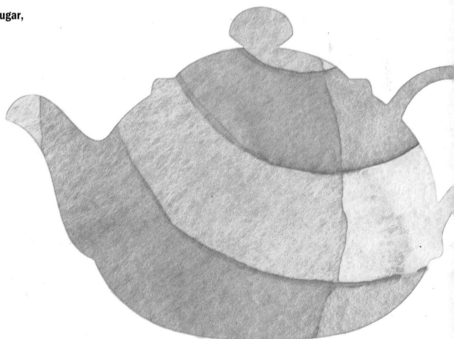

Peanut tea is a rich, comforting, frothy, dessert-like beverage that tastes like liquid peanut butter. I've dubbed this "hot peanut butter milk," since it actually doesn't contain any tea. I prefer it on the sweeter side, but please adjust the sweetener to suit your own taste.

ye'lewuz shai

PEANUT TEA AKA HOT PEANUT BUTTER MILK

MAKES 2 CUPS

1 cup **water**

1 cup **unsweetened plain vegan milk**

2 tablespoons **natural unsweetened creamy peanut butter**

2 tablespoons **agave nectar or other sweetener,** plus more if desired

Combine all the ingredients in a blender and process until smooth. Taste and add more agave nectar if desired. Pour into a medium saucepan and cook over medium-high heat, stirring frequently to prevent scorching, until hot.

Per cup: 200 calories, 8 g protein, 10 g fat (1.2 g sat), 21 g carbohydrates, 35 mg sodium, 150 mg calcium, 2 g fiber his drink is a real treat and tastes like a rich, creamy, nut-butter shake. The addition of a frozen banana makes it even creamier and more luscious. Traditionally, *telba* is made with just flaxseeds, water, and sugar or honey, but I prefer it fancied up a bit, as it is in this recipe.

telba

A ROASTED-FLAXSEED SHAKE

MAKES 3 TO 4 CUPS

2 cups **unsweetened plain vegan milk, cold**

1 cup **cold water**

⅓ cup **whole brown flaxseeds, toasted and ground into a powder** (see page 14)

2 tablespoons **agave nectar**

1 teaspoon **pure vanilla extract**

½ teaspoon **ground cinnamon**

1 **frozen banana** (optional)

Combine all the ingredients in a blender. Process until smooth and creamy. Serve immediately.

Per cup (based on 4 cups): 149 calories, 6 g protein, 7 g fat (0.2 g sat), 14 g carbohydrates, 39 mg sodium, 190 mg calcium, 5 g fiber

COOKING TIP: Sweeten this shake to taste with more or less agave nectar, stevia, pitted dates, or whatever other sweetener you prefer.

*T*hese cookies taste like a cross between snickerdoodles and coconut-lemon sugar cookies. They have a slight snap, with soft interiors and gently cracked tops. Be sure to let them rest for at least five minutes before eating, so they don't crumble into your coffee or tea (unless you want them to).

spiced teff snickerdoodles

MAKES 24 COOKIES

cookie dough

3 tablespoons **unsweetened plain vegan milk**

1 tablespoon **ground flaxseeds, any variety**

¾ cup **unbleached granulated sugar**

½ cup **melted unrefined coconut oil**

2 teaspoons **pure vanilla extract**

1 teaspoon **lemon zest**

1 cup **teff flour**

½ cup **sorghum flour**

⅓ cup **tapioca starch**

½ teaspoon **baking powder**

½ teaspoon **baking soda**

½ teaspoon **cream of tartar**

½ teaspoon **ground cinnamon**

¼ teaspoon **salt**

2 tablespoons **finely minced candied ginger,** for decoration

Preheat the oven to 350 degrees F. Line a baking sheet with parchment paper.

To make the cookie dough, put the vegan milk and flaxseeds in a small bowl and mix with a spoon until blended. Let rest until thickened, 5 to 10 minutes.

Put the ¾ cup of sugar and oil into the bowl of a stand mixer and beat on medium speed until well blended, about 1 minute. Add the thickened flax mixture, vanilla extract, and lemon zest and beat, stopping occasionally to scrape down the bowl, until smooth and creamy, about 1 minute.

Put the teff flour, sorghum flour, tapioca starch, baking powder, baking soda, cream of tartar, cinnamon, and salt in a medium bowl and stir to combine. Add the flour mixture to the flax mixture and beat until a soft dough forms. The dough will seem crumbly at first but will quickly come together.

⅓ cup **unbleached granulated sugar**

1 teaspoon **ground cinnamon**

⅛ teaspoon **ground cardamom**

Pinch **ground cloves**

To make the topping, put the sugar, cinnamon, cardamom, and cloves in a small baking pan or on a rimmed plate and stir to combine.

To form and bake the cookies, shape rounded tablespoons of the dough into 1-inch balls. Roll the balls in the topping, making sure they're well coated all over. Press a pinch of the candied ginger on top. Transfer the balls to the prepared baking sheet, arranging them at least two inches apart. Bake for 10 to 11 minutes, until the cookies flatten and spread slightly and tops are lightly cracked.

Let the cookies rest undisturbed for 5 minutes on the baking sheet, then carefully transfer them with a spatula to a wire rack. Let cool for at least 5 minutes longer. The cookies will be crumbly when hot but will firm as they cool. Store the cool cookies in a tightly closed container at room temperature for up to 4 days.

Per cookie: 114 calories, 1 g protein, 5 g fat (4 g sat), 17 g carbohydrates, 58 mg sodium, 16 mg calcium, 1 g fiber

mocha teff brownies

MAKES 12 BROWNIES

1⅓ cups **sorghum flour**

¼ cup **potato starch**

¼ cup **tapioca starch**

2½ teaspoons **baking powder**

½ teaspoon **salt**

1 cup **unbleached granulated sugar**

2 tablespoons **water**

1 cup **freshly brewed coffee**

⅓ cup **teff flour**

¼ cup **coconut oil** (refined or unrefined)

¼ cup **organic canola oil**

¾ cup **brown sugar, not packed**

⅔ cup **unsweetened cocoa powder**

2 tablespoons **finely ground flaxseeds** (any variety)

1 teaspoon **pure vanilla extract**

⅓ cup **vegan semisweet chocolate chips**

Preheat the oven to 350 degrees F. Line an 8-inch square glass baking pan with parchment paper.

Put the sorghum flour, potato starch, tapioca starch, baking powder, and salt in a medium bowl and stir to combine.

Put the granulated sugar and water in a small saucepan and stir to combine. Cook over medium-high heat, stirring almost constantly, until the sugar has mostly dissolved, about 6 minutes. Don't let the mixture boil. Transfer the hot mixture to the bowl of a stand mixer and rinse out the saucepan.

Combine the coffee and teff flour in the same saucepan and cook over medium-high heat, stirring constantly, until the mixture begins to bubble and thicken. Once the mixture is thick and smooth and the consistency of pudding, cook and stir for 1 minute longer. Transfer to the bowl with the sugar and add the coconut oil and canola oil. Beat with an electric mixer until smooth (be careful of splashes, as the mixture will be hot), about 1 minute.

Add the brown sugar, cocoa powder, flaxseeds, and vanilla extract and beat until creamy and smooth, about 2 minutes.

Slowly add in the flour mixture and beat, stopping occasionally to scrape down the beaters and the sides of the bowl, until the batter is thick and smooth, about 2 minutes. Stir in the chocolate chips.

Scrape the batter into the prepared baking pan using a rubber spatula. Spread the batter evenly, making sure to get it in all corners. Smooth the top. Bake for 35 to 40 minutes, until the brownies have risen, the top is shiny and set, and the edges and corners are firm.

Cool to room temperature. Cut into squares or rectangles.

Per brownie: 310 calories, 4 g protein, 13 g fat (6 g sat), 49 g carbohydrates, 111 mg sodium, 48 mg calcium, 4 g fiber

Mocha-Nut Brownies: Add ½ cup of chopped pecans, walnuts, or hazelnuts along with the chocolate chips.

Rocky Road Brownies: Replace the chocolate chips with 5 ounces of chopped vegan marshmallows.

ACKNOWLEDGMENTS

ursha is the Ethiopian tradition of wrapping a little morsel of the choicest foods in *injera* and popping it into the mouths of special friends, loved ones, and family as a sign of honor, love, and respect. If distance didn't separate me from all the wonderful people who have contributed and helped me with this book, I'd reach over and give you each a giant *gursha*. Especially, I would like to thank the following: Amy Gedgaudas, Anson Berns, Anthony Kinik, Cynthia Combs, Dave Cash, Eric Smith, Erika Larson, Fikre Yibsa, Gabrielle Pope, Hirut Yibsa, Jacqueline Smith, Jennie Harned, John Plummer, Julie Hasson (and her infamous steamed seitan method), Kim Cannard, Lori D., Mesfin Hailemariam, Michelle Citrin, Michelle Schwegman, Miyoko Schinner, Paul Gailiunas, Sarah Kramer, and Wendy Berns (my sweet mama).

To the Portland, Oregon, Ethiopian businesses that kept my belly and pantry full while I worked on this project: Merkato Ethiopian Music and Food Store, Awash Market, Bete Lukas Ethiopian Restaurant, and Emame's Ethiopian Cuisine.

The recipes in this book were put through their paces by an amazing squad of enthusiastic, thorough, and dedicated people. Testing recipes is no easy task, and I'm especially grateful to all of you for your passion, time, and commitment to this project. Thank you for making me feel confident about these recipes: Abby Bean and 89, Amber Powell, Andrea Zeichner, Camille Carter, Chel Rabbit, Chris Timmons, Crystal Carter, Dave Cash, Emily Berna, Erika Larson, Erin Goddard, Jacqueline Smith, Jennifer Busby, Jesse Ives and Katie Marggraf, Katie Hay, Lauren Saliba, Lisa Higgins, Liz Lew, Liz Wyman, Michelle Citrin, Monika Soria Caruso, Rachel Strasser, Renae Myers, Steffers Christianson, and especially the most amazingly helpful and unstoppable Susan Antoniewicz.

The last thank-you is saved for my best friend and partner, David Koen (aka Dazee), for believing in me and my cooking, and for pushing and encouraging me to make this book a reality (even if it turned Vee into an irrevocable *injera* junkie).

Lokah samastah sukhino bhavantu.

May all creatures everywhere be at peace and free from suffering.

RESOURCES AND SUPPLIERS

AMY'S MERKATO

amysmerkato.com

Amy's Merkato is a small grocery in Seattle, Washington, specializing in Ethiopian spices and ingredients. They also make *injera* on site and will ship if you call them directly. Their gluten-free, 100 percent teff *injera* is prepared on demand, with twenty-four hour's notice.

BOB'S RED MILL

bobsredmill.com

Bob's Red Mill is an accessible source for many hard-to-find flours, legumes, and starches, including brown teff flour, sorghum flour, oat flour, chickpea flour, tapioca starch, and potato starch. The website offers a store locator service, and many well-stocked supermarkets and natural food stores carry their products. I've noticed that in stores the gluten-free flours are often stocked in a separate aisle from their other products, so be sure to ask for help if you have trouble locating a specific product.

BRUNDO

brundo.com

Brundo is a grocery store in Oakland, California, specializing in Ethiopian spices and ingredients. They import from their own factory in Ethiopia, make *injera* on site, and also offer vegan Ethiopian cooking classes.

ETHIOPIAN SPICES

ethiopianspices.com

Ethiopian Spices is a small importer of Ethiopian spices and ingredients. They stock a wide variety of ingredients as well as fresh injera.

HOW TO COOK GREAT ETHIOPIAN FOOD

howtocookgreatethiopian.com

How to Cook Great Ethiopian Food is an online resource with invaluable information on Ethiopian ingredients and cooking videos.

MESOB ACROSS AMERICA

ethiopianfood.wordpress.com

Mesob Across America is a blog about Ethiopian Food written by Harry Kloman. This site is an amazing resource for reading about the history and culture of Ethiopian food. It also provides other very useful information including recipes, an extensive restaurant list with links by state, cooking video links, and cookbook reviews.

PURCELL MOUNTAIN FARMS

purcellmountainfarms.com

Purcell Mountain Farms is an online retailer of spices, grains, legumes, and flours. They are one of the few suppliers of domestically grown, GMO-free ivory and brown Maskal teff flour. They also carry the small brown fava beans (marrone bell peas) needed for *Shehan Ful* (page 46).

SHILOH FARMS

shilohfarms.com

Shiloh Farms is an online supplier of grains, flours, and legumes. They also stock both ivory and brown domestic teff flours along with lentils and split peas.

TEFFCO

teffco.com

Teffco is an online supplier of domestically grown, GMO-free ivory and brown Maskal teff flour. They also stock green Ethiopian coffee beans, if you want to roast your own beans at home.

VEGAN ETHIOPIA

facebook.com/veganethiopia
twitter.com/veganethiopia

PO Box 28305/1000
Addis Ababa, Ethiopia

Vegan Ethiopia is a small organization in Addis Ababa that is focused on vegan advocacy, education, and animal rights.

VITACOST

vitacost.com

Vitacost is an online supplier specializing in natural groceries and vitamins. They stock brown and ivory teff flour, sorghum flour, tapioca starch, and potato starch. In addition, they carry canned organic fava beans, spices, roasted Ethiopian coffee beans, and several commercial brands of ground *berbere*. They also stock West Soy unsweetened organic soy milk.

WESTBRAE NATURAL

westbrae.com
westsoymilk.com

Westbrae Natural offers organic beans, including white and fava beans, in BPA-free cans. They also produce an unsweetened organic soy milk, made with only soybeans and water, under their West Soy label. These products are widely available in well-stocked supermarkets and natural food stores.

ABOUT THE AUTHOR

KITTEE BERNS loves food. She especially loves sharing food with friends, learning about new recipes and techniques, and talking about food with anyone who cares to chat. She's the author of the vegan cookzine *Papa Tofu Loves Ethiopian Food* and the creative force behind the blog Cake Maker to the Stars. Her recipes have appeared in several books and publications, including *Vegan Pizza*, *Vegan Pie in the Sky*, *The Vegan Girl's Guide to Life*, *Let Gluten Freedom Ring*, and *Hungry Monkey*.

Kittee has been an ethical vegan for over twenty-four years and a gluten-free vegan since 2008. She has over thirteen years experience in the natural foods industry. Besides obsessing over vegan cooking and food, Kittee enjoys thrifting, digging through estate sales, gardening, collecting vintage dishware and fabrics, and making things by hand. She currently resides in the veganopolis of Portland, Oregon, with her partner, Dazee, and their dog, Vee Seven. Follow her online at kitteekake.blogspot.com.

INDEX